APPENDIX

1 – ADDRESS LIST – 89
2 – RIGGING TOPOS – 90

INTRODUCTION

This small book, despite its title, is obviously not a comprehensive instructional manual of vertical caving techniques – such a book would contain many hundreds of pages and require some very determined reading. The current book is but one of a series outlining the latest caving techniques and equipment.

Although some basic equipment and techniques are described for completeness, neither is the book aimed at the beginner – there are already too many such books. But rather as a handbook for the fairly experienced caver interested in developing his technical skills. With such a subject it's hard to know where to begin – and even harder where to stop. The general approach has been to provide background information describing the main characteristics of the equipment used, followed by a section detailing the techniques of using it.

The principles of vertical caving are easily understood; the practice requires proper training, close attention to prevailing circumstances and constant modification of acquired techniques in the light of new information and equipment. Unfortunately with caving there are some mistakes you can make only once! The aim of this small book is simply to help overcome the technical problems of rigging and climbing pitches in order to experience the underworld in safety.

We should then keep it firmly in mind that the ultimate value of the cave environment and the privileged time spent there, lies not in its scientific importance or ecological significance, and least of all as a dangerous proving ground for cavers. But simply the fact that it is a cave – deep and dark and fascinating.

WARNING – CAVING IS DANGEROUS

The equipment and techniques described in this book are employed in circumstances where the safety of the user is at risk. It is the caver's responsibility at all times to ensure that he understands the safe and correct use of the equipment and techniques involved. Accordingly, the author and publishers cannot accept responsibility for damage or injury resulting from misuse of equipment or misunderstanding of the advice given in this book.

1– VERTICAL EQUIPMENT

1 — VERTICAL EQUIPMENT

1.1 KARABINERS 7
General Considerations
Care of Karabiners

1.2 MAILLON RAPIDES 9
Applications

1.3 HARNESS 10
Function
General Considerations
Sit-Harness
Design
Material
Choosing a Harness
Chest-Harness
Design

1.4 SAFETY-CORDS 13
Function
General Considerations
Fabrication
Care and Maintenance

1.5 DESCENDERS 16
Function/Principles
Choice of Descender
"Simple" Descender
"Auto-Lock" Descender

1.6 JAMMERS 18
Function
Types
Sprung-Cam Jammers/Principle
Description
Maintenance

1.7 FOOTLOOPS 21
Description

1.8 PULLEYS 22
Function
Types

1.9 TACKLE SACKS 23
Function
Design
"Standard" Sacks
"Special Purpose" Sacks

1 — VERTICAL EQUIPMENT

This section describes the basic SRT equipment and outlines its capabilities, some understanding of which is essential to safe use.

1.1 KARABINERS

Karabiners are versatile metal links with an opening in one side, the "gate", closed by a sprung "keeper", which may be secured by a screwed sleeve. Screwgate karabiners are generally preferred for cave use where security is more important than speed of attachment. Where considered unnecessary, the sleeve is simply left unfastened, or better still, screwed back out of the way.

GENERAL CONSIDERATIONS

Karabiners are available in both steel and aluminium alloys in a multitude of shapes and sizes. In general, any karabiner with a breaking load of around 2000kg is suitable for use underground.

Steel karabiners are harder wearing than alloy and so withstand regular cave usage better, although in any quantity they are prohibitively heavy. Alloy karabiners, while equally strong, are considerably lighter but require more care in use. Running a dirty rope over an alloy karabiner, for instance, will soon wear and weaken it.

All karabiners are strongest loaded along their "major axis" (end to end) and very much weaker if loaded sideways across the gate or "minor axis" Here the load is inevitably transferred to the 2/3mm dia. hinge pin, which results in failure at much lower levels.

The shape of a karabiner determines the way it carries a load. With oval-shaped karabiners (Fig-1) the load is shared equally between the gated and ungated sides. Assymetric (e.g. offset D-shaped) karabiners (Fig-2) are designed to support a greater

8

proportion of the load on the spine, which is considerably stronger than the gated side. This however, is not always completely borne out in practice, particularly where two or three ropes in the same karabiner may cause it to be loaded much closer to the gate. Conversely, because a larger proportion of the load is taken on the spine, assymetric karabiners may be opened under higher loads than the equivalent oval type, an advantage in certain circumstances.

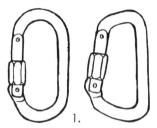

Figs-1.2.3.4. - Types of Karabiner.

1.   2.   3.   4.

The type of latch securing the keeper is also important. The strength of a "latch and pin" type catch (Fig-3) remains more or less the same whether or not the sleeve is screwed up, although of course its intrinsic security will be lessened. With the somewhat outdated "cross" type latch (Fig-4.) the karabiner may reach only 50% of its quoted breaking load if the sleeve is not fastened. Nowadays, this type of karabiner is best avoided altogether.

Under very muddy conditions, clogging of the latch may prevent the keeper from automatically closing properly. In this condition, both types of gate are equally weak if the latch is not engaged and the karabiner acts simply as a hook, reaching perhaps only 25% of its maximum breaking load.

Bear in mind also that any figures relating to breaking load apply to new karabiners; manufacturers do not test old karabiners and not one gets any stronger with wear.

> Avoid incorrect loading. In any situation where substantial 3-way loading is likely to unduly stress the gate, a karabiner is unsafe. For example, certain types of harness have a central connection which serves to link the harness together and also acts as the main attachment point. Here a karabiner is insufficient and a sturdy Maillon Rapide far safer.

CARE OF KARABINERS

Routine maintenance consists of washing off mud. When dry, a squirt of spray lubricant (WD40) will keep the hinge operating freely and help prevent the internal spring rusting. Grease is not so good as particles of grit tend to stick to it which somewhat defeats the object.

Regularly inspect karabiners and discard them if at all suspect - do it conscientiously, your life depends on it. Any worn or damaged karabiners should be broken and disposed of rather than relegated to non-critical uses such as tackle hauling, digging or carrying ammo-cans. If kept, such karabiners inevitably find their way back into the system when gear runs short on a trip, and are then potentially lethal.

1.2 MAILLON RAPIDES

Maillon Rapides (M/Rs) are solid metal links closed by a sturdy threaded sleeve and so capable of supporting a load applied in any direction without significant loss of strength. They are produced in both stainless and plated steel in various shapes and a wide range of sizes. The different sizes are referred to according to the diameter of the metal rod from which they are formed. Certain of the larger sizes are also manufactured in aluminium alloy.

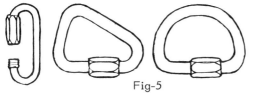
Fig-5

Maillon Rapides - Sturdy industrial fittings made for linking chain. Useful in certain situations to replace a karabiner.

APPLICATIONS

In caving for the most part, only a few specific types are required (Fig-5). The 7mm dia. long-series oval type (plated steel) is used for rigging in place of karabiners. The long-series has a wider gate opening than the "standard" model, which allows the rope to be inserted more easily. A 10mm dia. "Delta" or "Semi-circular" type forms the main attachment point at the front of the harness and a 10mm dia. long-series oval may be used to attach the descender - all of these are aluminium alloy. Alloy M/Rs should be regularly inspected for wear.

Maillon Rapides can be used underground whenever a strong, secure fastening is required that need not be opened and closed frequently. They are, however, extremely weak if the sleeve is not screwed up. Moreover, even very slight loading in this condition will distort the body sufficiently to prevent the sleeve from subsequently being properly fastened. While screwing the sleeve up fingertight is usually adequate, use of a small spanner allows this to be tightened sufficiently for safety and yet easily released. In any case, it is necessary to carry a spanner to deal with the occasional stiff sleeve.

A 13mm A/F spanner for 8mm bolts more or less fits 7mm dia. M/Rs. The distance between the sides of a 7mm dia. M/R (i.e. 16mm) corresponds exactly to the sleeve of a 10mm dia. M/R and can be used as a makeshift spanner. Alternatively, the simple alloy spanner shown (Fig-6) fits both and also the hexagonal gate sleeves of certain karabiners.

Fig-6

Mini-Spanner for
7 & 10mm Ø M/Rs.

1.3 HARNESS

FUNCTION

A caver's harness is his sole means of suspension from the rope, he cannot effectively attach himself without it – the harness is as necessary as the rope itself. In this regard, its function is to distribute his bodyweight (and any shock-loading) around the upper thigh and pelvic region where it is most safely and comfortably supported. In practical terms, the harness arrangement must also maintain the caver in a relatively upright attitude, permit the range of movements needed to climb the rope, and not unduly hinder general progress through the cave. Clearly the harness must be strong and secure enough to sustain the forces developed in arresting a fall. Moreover, because the harness is commonly worn throughout the caving trip, it should be durable enough to withstand repeated harsh use and yet remain safe.

(Of course in order to gain acceptance amongst older club cavers, it should also weigh nothing, last forever, and the caver must be able to make it himself from old inner tubes and Araldite!)

GENERAL CONSIDERATIONS

A one-piece full-body harness is the safest type, except that current models designed for mountaineering are cumbersome, over

elaborate and ill suited to rope climbing techniques. In caving, the most common arrangement is a combination of separate sit and chest-harness where the sit-harness is the basic means of support and the chest-harness serves to tow a body-mounted jammer whilst helping to keep the caver upright on the rope (Fig-7).
It is important to stress that any chest-harness be used only in conjunction with a sit-harness, the two solidly linked together so that the major part of any load is transmitted directly to the sit-harness. Effectively hanging from a chest-harness alone can be extremely dangerous, compression of the rib cage leading to unconsciousness and death within a very short period.

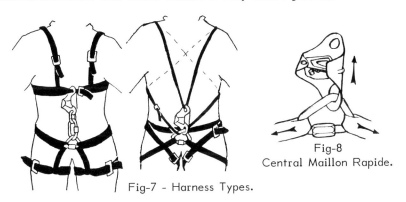

Fig-8
Central Maillon Rapide.

Fig-7 - Harness Types.

Equally important is that where the main attachment point at the front of the harness is also used to fasten the harness together, this should not consist of a karabiner. This position is inevitably subject to a 3-way loading, very likely to stress the gate section of the karabiner which is its weakest point. The harness is linked with a screw-sleeved Maillon Rapide (Fig-8), which is not only far stronger, but may be loaded in any direction without significant loss of strength. One further precaution is to arrange the M/R with the sleeve at the bottom so that the result is not disastrous should this accidently work loose. A small alloy spanner (see Fig−6.) allows the sleeve to be tightened sufficiently to obviate this possibility and yet be easily released whenever necessary.

SIT-HARNESS

Although there are many types of sit-harness available, the most suitable are those with individual leg-loops and an integral belt section. There is an important distinction between a caver's sit-harness (with its low attachment point for efficient rope climbing and designed to allow maximum leg movement while suspended) and a rock-climber's sit-harness. The latter is designed to minimise the effects of a fall and uses a higher attachment to keep the (fallen) climber upright and help assume a safe sitting position. However, the low attachment point of a caver's harness means that without some support from a chest-harness, the caver losing his balance is in danger of hanging upside down.

DESIGN

For comfort, the harness should be constructed of laterally rigid webbing which remains flat and spreads the load over a wide surface area. The "belt" section is better resting on the rigid pelvic girdle rather than acting to compress the soft internal organs around the waist. With a male caver, the leg loop straps must obviously avoid any adjacent external "soft organs" entirely and should also be easily adjustable to allow for slackening off in horizontal stretches of cave. A lightweight retaining strap at the rear prevents the loops slipping down behind the thighs while stooping or crawling. The sit-harness is worn more or less all the time underground and if well designed, does not hinder movement; on the contrary, it keeps the oversuit in place and ensures freedom for the legs. Narrow webbing loops on the belt section are useful for carrying small items of equipment and do not, unlike karabiners, dig painfully into the hip bone. Finally, it is vitally important that all load-bearing stitching and any tie-in points are adequately protected from abrasion.

MATERIAL

Harnesses are invariably made from either Nylon (Polyamide) or Terylene (Polyester) webbing. Both are excellent harness materials, more or less equally strong and abrasion resistant, but unfortunately susceptible to serious damage arising from corrosive chemicals used in the mining lamp accumulators once favoured by British cavers. Such batteries are carried on a belt in close contact with the harness and the insidious threat of contamination by a leaking battery is ever present. The situation is slightly complicated in that Nylon is severely weakened by the acid electrolyte used in "Oldham" type cells, whereas Terylene is most readily affected by the strong alkaline electrolyte of obsolete "Nife" type cells. Conversely, Nylon is resistant to alkaline and Terylene to acid, but not entirely so and in either case the only safe solution is to avoid absolutely any such contamination simply by using a more suitable lamp.

CHOOSING A HARNESS

No harness will match every caver's needs exactly and even amongst the most suitable types only comparative trials determine which model best suits a particular anatomy. Where possible, we would suggest borrowing different types from fellow cavers and trying them out underground. Keep abreast of the latest designs and buy a new harness only after trying it on and hanging from it for a while - where this facility is not provided, you can be sure you are in the wrong shop.

CHEST-HARNESS

The chest-harness serves two main purposes: it tows the body-mounted jammer up the rope while climbing and to some extent holds the climber erect when he stops. This latter feature, compromised in a caver's harness, is nonetheless essential for safety reasons - in the case of an accident or exhaustion on a pitch, it prevents the unfortunate victim from turning upside down and allows a relatively comfortable rest position.

DESIGN

There are many types available corresponding to different tastes and needs. Climbing the rope the chest-harness supports a proportion of the weight of the tackle sack relieving the load on the belt, and also aids direct lifting methods during rescue and hauling manoeuvres. The harness should be readily adjustable and fitted with a quick-release buckle/s which can be quickly tightened for efficient climbing, but easily slackened off when required - in a sloping pitch, for example, or for comfort in horizontal galleries.

1.4 SAFETY-CORDS

The safety-cords (cows-tails) consist of a length of rope attached to the main M/R so as to leave one short length and another somewhat longer, each with a karabiner at its end (see Fig-42 p.38)

FUNCTION

The use of these simple devices is extremely varied, but essentially they are used to hang from during certain manoeuvres

14

and as a safeguard against falling in others. They provide a strong means of attachment for protection in hazardous places, such as gaining the rope at a pitch head or passing a rebelay point. With modern rigging techniques, it's virtually impossible to progress safely without them.

GENERAL CONSIDERATIONS

It might appear on the face of it that a length of sturdy cord capable of supporting the weight of an average caver, multiplied two or three times in order to provide a safety factor, would be sufficiently strong. Consequently, almost any old bit of cord or tape might seem adequate; however, this is certainly far from the truth. A caver's safety-cords are most necessary in situations where he might fall, and in doing so create a substantial shock-load. Here the safety-cord must not only withstand these forces without breaking, but must do so without transmitting an exaggerated shock-load to the caver or his anchor. For example, safety-cords of inelastic wire cable, while more than strong enough, would be very dangerous (for the principles of shock absorption - see p.47). Tape webbing, particularly Polyester webbing, is also not good. Tape has a limited shock absorption capacity and due to a proportionately large surface area relative to its mass, is prone to rapid weakening from wear. If sufficiently thick and strong, tape will not break, but will nevertheless transmit unnecessarily high forces to both caver and belay.

Even without delving into fall-factors (see p.47) or attempting to evaluate the hundreds of imaginary situations that arise at pitch heads, it's clear that a caver's safety-cords should be capable of handling falls of roughly the same order for which dynamic climbing ropes are designed. We need look no further - such ropes are hard wearing, flexible and subject to stringent manufacturing standards (see UIAA Standards), but are relatively cheap and come in lots of pretty colours. As to size - 9mm dia. climbing rope provides us with the right level of safety (2xFF2 falls) with minimum weight and bulk. Knots tied in 11mm dia. rope are much more bulky and the additional weight and bulk of the thicker rope useless.

FABRICATION

Safety-cords are often home-made, tied from 2.5 metres of rope using Fig.-8 Loops and ideally fitted with assymetric form karabiners rather than oval ones. The shorter cord is about 40/45cms long, including the karabiner. The longer one is less critical, but should not be so long that the karabiner is out of reach while hanging from it, say 65/70cms.

Because these karabiners are rarely attached for long, non-locking snaplinks are sometimes preferred. A screw sleeve on a karabiner, however, weighs virtually nothing and the security it provides is occasionally very welcome, although you don't always have to screw it up unless needed.

Safety-cords are most used in exposed and hazardous locations where often only one hand is free to manipulate them. Here fixed karabiners are always the right way round which minimises any fumbling and also ensures the correct end-to-end loading (Fig-9). Special "captive" karabiners are available with a removable bar at one end, or the karabiner can be simply fixed in place with a sturdy rubber band. Heat-shrink sleeving or binding the ends entirely with adhesive tape serves the same purpose and also protects the knot from abrasion damage.

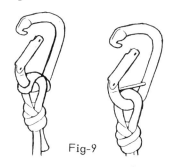

Fig-9

Captive Safety-Cord Karabiner.

A useful method of protecting the central attachment loop from undue wear is to sleeve it with a short section of sheath (about 10cms) taken from a thicker rope (11mm dia. for 9mm dia.). This is threaded onto the thinner rope and secured by tying it into the knot. All knots should be well tightened before use by loading with body-weight and bouncing up and down.

CARE AND MAINTENANCE

A caver's safety-cords accompany him everywhere. They are loyal friends and in return are subjected to fairly harsh treatment. Following each trip they must be washed and carefully inspected for damage. It is important to replace them whenever they become appreciably worn or following a shock-load. In common with all ropes, they are also weakened simply by the effects of age. So in any case, renew them at least once each year. Make a regular date for this - while checking equipment after a winter lay-up or when preparing for a summer expedition. The cost of replacement is negligible and a small price to pay for continued peace of mind.

1.5 DESCENDERS

FUNCTION/PRINCIPLES

Abseiling refers to the technique of sliding down a fixed rope under full control. This is made possible by use of a descender, which is simply a brake or friction device that converts movement energy to heat. The heat produced is dissipated into the surrounding air by both the descender and the rope.

In use, the rope is threaded through the descender attached to the sit-harness. The caver then grips the rope beneath the descender more or less firmly, providing the additional tension needed to control the descent.

The braking power of a particular device is a function of the friction created between it and the rope. This varies considerably for a given rope according to whether it is wet, dry, or muddy, and is largely determined by tension in the rope beneath, partly from the caver gripping the rope and also the weight of free rope hanging below. Much of the skill of abseiling lies in compensating for these variables and effecting a smooth, controlled descent.

CHOICE OF DESCENDER

There are many different descenders of one sort or another; manufacturers of mountaineering equipment are particularly prolific in this field, but only two types are considered suitable for these techniques. These are the "Dressler" (Fig-11) and "Rack" (Fig-10) type devices, both specifically designed for SRT although with somewhat differing criteria. Within the context of the techniques described, the Dressler type descenders (particularly auto-lock models) are more effective than Rack designs on almost all counts apart from ease of control on extremely long pitches – over 100 metres say. Since pitches are, for various reasons (speed, safety – see p. 78) usually split into sections much shorter than this, the Rack can be considered as rather less suitable for general use and is discussed no further.

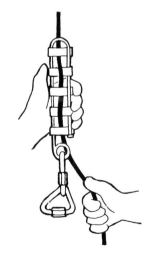

Fig-10 - Rack Descender.

"SIMPLE" DESCENDER

The Dressler descender (simple model) is the standard device adopted by most European cavers (Fig-11.). It comprises of two fixed bollards secured with bolts between alloy side plates. One side plate is pivoted and provided with an oval attachment hole, open at one side and fitted with a sprung safety catch. This arrangement allows the side plate to rotate, enabling the rope to be introduced without unfastening the descender from the harness. The rope path describes an S-shape around the bollards, providing sufficient friction without twisting the rope. The rope is also run through a steel "braking" karabiner positioned between the descender and the "controlling" hand, which aids control and facilitates "locking-off" (see p. 30). In isolated cases, with unusually thick ropes or those swollen with mud, it is possible to reduce the braking effect by threading the rope around the outside of the bollards in the form of a "C" rather than the usual "S" (Fig-12). However, this technique is rarely necessary and must always be used with extreme caution. The Simple descender can be used either left or right-handed.

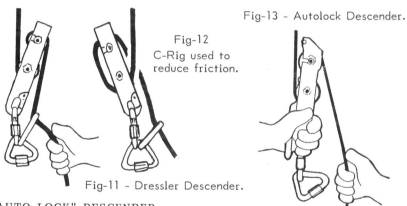

Fig-13 - Autolock Descender.

Fig-12
C-Rig used to reduce friction.

Fig-11 - Dressler Descender.

"AUTO-LOCK" DESCENDER

With almost any descender, the rate of descent is controlled by the caver's grip tensioning the rope beneath. Losing control is always a possibility since positive action on the part of the caver is required to slow the descent. Should he let go for any reason (mistake, panic, injury), the descent becomes a more or less free fall and the landing more or less disastrous.

A comparatively recent development of the basic descender is an "auto-lock" adaptation (Fig-13). Such descenders have an integral handle which when operated allows the device to function more or less as a conventional descender. Releasing the handle, however, causes an eccentric cam to lock onto the rope and halt the descent - inaction (letting go) becomes safer. This feature aids locking-off the descender manually during manoeuvres, and also to some extent acts as a "failsafe" in an emergency. Let go of the handle for whatever reason, the descent stops and subsequently is easily resumed.

It should be noted that in certain very tight pitches, it may not be possible to operate the handle properly. For this reason there must always be some provision for preventing the descender locking when this function is not required. Obviously the descender must then be locked-off and released manually.

The auto-lock concept is a major advancement in terms of safety and convenience; these descenders are the only type considered in this book. However, one inherent disadvantage of existing designs arises from the necessity of releasing the handle for the device to lock onto the rope. A thoughtless or panicking caver might instinctively react by gripping the handle tighter, which only worsens the situation. Nevertheless, this disadvantage can be adequately overcome by suitable training.

1.6 JAMMERS

FUNCTION

Central to any rope climbing or hauling system are one-way jamming devices which will slide easily along the fixed rope, then lock firmly and not slide back. All jammers utilise the same basic principle, that of a cam trapping the rope against the body of the device when a directional load is applied.

TYPES

There are many such devices, each with its own characteristics, but they can be classified into just two groups according to the principle used to operate the cam.

1. Those where the load is taken on the body of the jammer and the toothed cam is initially operated by a spring (Sprung-Cam Jammers),

2. Those where the load is applied directly to the pivoted cam by lever action, with or without a spring to close the cam (Lever-Cam Jammers).

Fig-14

Fig-15

1. SPRUNG-CAM JAMMERS

    A. Petzl Jammers
    B. Jumar
    C. Kong Ventrali Jammer

2. LEVER-CAM JAMMERS

    D. Kong Handled Jammer
    E. Gibbs Ropewalker
    F. Shunt

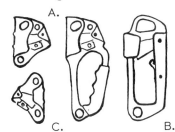

By and large all jammers are interchangeable, but the grip on the rope differs in each case and, to an extent, the design of a particular device determines its best use. For example, sprung-cam devices rely on the toothed face of the cam to engage the surface of the rope and may slip on muddy or icy ropes, or if excessively worn, whereas lever-cam jammers do not. However, most lever-cam devices tilt when loaded which results in a small loss of height gain. Also due to the principle involved, such jammers normally have only a single attachment point which limits their application.

Because of their suitability to the techniques employed, the descriptions in this book refer entirely to sprung-cam jammers. Those described are all mechanically identical but feature certain modifications to the body-shape designed to fit a particular role.

SPRUNG-CAM JAMMERS - PRINCIPLE

The rope is confined to a U-shaped channel with the cam held lightly against it by a spring. The face of the cam has small spikes which engage the surface of the rope as the jammer is loaded and so cause the cam to turn, compressing the rope against the back of the channel and firmly locking the device. With all sprung-cam jammers the load is applied to the body. Typically this is provided with at least two points of load-bearing attachment, which adds to its versatility in use.

DESCRIPTION

The "Standard" jammer (Fig-16.) consists of a formed sheet duraluminium body fitted with a plated steel cam. The cam face has small downward pointing teeth to ease sliding up the rope and improve the grip when initially loaded. A sprung safety catch prevents the rope escaping accidently in use and in a second position allows the cam to be held open while the rope is introduced. This jammer is generally loaded from the single hole at its base, although twin holes provided in the upper section of the body are favoured by some cavers and are also used for self-lining. By clipping a karabiner into these holes and around the rope, the strength and security of the jammer is increased, but this is awkward to use and seldom adopted in practice. A further hole in the rear upper section of the jammer allows it to be mounted on the body harness if necessary. Together with a compatible pulley and karabiners, the jammer forms a versatile pulley-jammer unit (see p. 88) with many hauling and rescue applications. One (right-handed) model only.

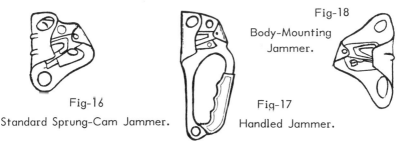

Fig-18
Body-Mounting
Jammer.

Fig-16
Standard Sprung-Cam Jammer.

Fig-17
Handled Jammer.

The "Handled" jammer (Fig-17.) is virtually identical to the Standard jammer but with an integral plastic-coated handle. Mainly used by mountaineers, it is preferred by some cavers for rope climbing and useful when a firm grip is called for, tackle hauling for instance. Manufactured in both left and right-handed versions, it can be body-mounted if required.

The "Body-mounted" jammer (Fig-18.) is also similar in most respects but specifically designed to be attached directly to the harness as part of a rope climbing rig. The frame is twisted to encourage it to lie flat and the cut-away profile of the front section permits the rope to be taken in and out more easily. Certain models have slots in the cam face which help prevent clogging with mud. Others have a modified safety catch to minimise the chance of this being accidently released in use. Two attachment holes, one at each end of the body, facilitate mounting between sit and chest-harnesses. The lower hole is large enough to pass the gate sleeve of a 10mm dia. M/R and positioned some distance from the edge to allow for the wear that occurs at this point. One (right-handed) model only.

MAINTENANCE

Maintenance of jammers is limited to washing and drying, inspecting the frame for sharp edges (caused by dirty ropes) which may cut the rope, and the face of the cam for undue wear (which will cause it to slip). Occasionally the springs and pivots should be lightly oiled, or better still, sprayed with a silicone lubricant such as WD40.

1.7 FOOTLOOPS

The footloop cord is necessary for climbing rope with jammers. Suspended from the upper jammer with a loop provided for the feet, the caver stands in this to raise himself.

DESCRIPTION

Generally a home-made item, best tied using Overhand and Bowline knots from a single length of 8mm dia. low-stretch rope (Fig-19.). Webbing should be avoided, it wears rapidly and has a tendency to catch in the body-jammer while climbing. The footloop itself is secured with a Bowline for ease of adjustment and the loop made large enough (40cms) to take both boots. This is useful when climbing a free-hanging pitch and also aids trapping the rope between the boots for the initial few metres so that no-one is needed to hold it.

Fig-19

Combined footloop and safety link of 8/9mm dia. Nylon rope.

A screwgate karabiner is used to attach the central (Overhand) knot to the upper jammer. The overall length of the footloop section is adjusted so that the two jammers almost touch when the legs are fully straightened (Fig-19.). The remaining section of cord acts as a safety "tie-in", linking the upper jammer to the central point of the harness. This is attached to the bottom of the main Delta M/R with a karabiner or suitable M/R so that it can be easily detached without unfastening the harness. The length of this section is less critical, but should be long enough to permit the maximum step with each climbing cycle, yet not so long that the jammer is entirely out of reach while hanging from it.

1.8 PULLEYS

Although not an essential item of equipment, small, lightweight pulleys do prove useful in a number of isolated situations, e.g. tackle hauling, use on tyroleans or guide ropes, and in rescue/hauling applications.

FUNCTION

The function of a pulley is simply that of reducing friction where a rope is pulled through an acute angle. While the lightweight designs manufactured for caving are comparatively poor in this respect, nevertheless they still make a number of tasks that much easier.

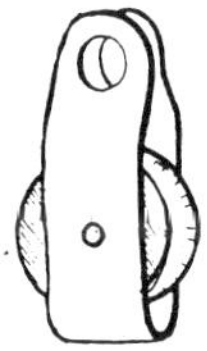

Fig-21 - Strap Pulley.

Fig-20 - Swing-Cheek Pulley.

Fig-22
Karabiner Pulley Wheel.

TYPES

There are various types, the most common based on either "Swing-cheek" (Fig-20.) or "Strap" designs (Fig-21.). Both are constructed with alloy side plates and plastic wheels and designed to be introduced onto the mid-part of a rope without access to its ends. A strap type pulley combined with a Standard jammer and two compatible karabiners makes an efficient pulley/jammer unit (see p. 88). The simplest pulley of all consists of a hard Nylon pulley wheel clipped directly into a round section karabiner (Fig-22.). This is much less efficient than a normal pulley, but then doesn't weigh a great deal either (15g).

1.9 TACKLE SACKS

FUNCTION

At its most basic the caver's tackle sack serves both to protect and facilitate the transport of rope and other necessary equipment through the cave. The protection of safety equipment is vital but, in addition, with the substantial amounts of gear needed for the longer and deeper explorations, it becomes important that this be moved through the cave with minimum inconvenience. To this end, the design of a tackle sack is of consequence, and while not directly related to safety, carrying a badly designed sack is frustrating, considerably slower and consequently more tiring.

DESIGN

Basic requirements of a tackle sack are that it be light, tough and rotproof, easily packed and fastened, with provision for carrying, dragging through difficult passages, and hauling up pitches. Desirable features include it being "streamlined" (snagproof) on the outside, free-standing for ease of packing, and brightly coloured so as not to get "lost" in muddy conditions. Considerations of shape and capacity are important: too bulky and the sack gets stuck in narrow passages, too small and it doesn't hold enough rope. Even in a roomy cave an over-large sack is difficult to manage, particularly if stuffed full of wet rope.

"STANDARD" SACKS

Lacking "standard" caves, there is need of different sacks for specific jobs. It makes sense where possible to relate their size and shape to the characteristics of the cave. For instance, a long, thin sack might be necessary for a particularly tight cave, and one with twin shoulder straps where a good deal of scrambling is involved, in order to leave both hands free (Fig-23.).

Fig 23
Standard
Twin-Strap
Tackle Sack

Fig-24
Large Capacity
Tackle Sack.

In general, a tubular or oval shape is preferred - there is no right or wrong side up and no protruding corners to wear

through. The design and construction of the sack is important
and an extremely tough, abrasion resistant fabric necessary.

Given a practical basic design and durable construction, the
sack must still be carried. British cave passages are normally so
tortuous that carrying straps are never exactly where you want
them to be. Nevertheless, all sacks need some provision for
carrying over the shoulder, and also a "grip" type handle part
way along the sack (somewhere about the point of balance), for
carrying the sack horizontally in low passages.

For dragging along crawls and hauling up pitches, twin
hauling loops - one on each side of the sack are necessary so that
the sack is held both vertical and closed while suspended, with
little to snag when being hauled against a wall. A useful feature
is a fastening system that is workable with gloved hands and also
allows access into the sack while it is suspended, in short, a
simple cord tie. Other features include an inner flap of some sort
so that small, loose items are kept secure, and an attached hauling
cord that floats (polypropylene) to aid recovery from deep pools.

In wet caves, large drain holes in the base of the sack avoid
carrying litres of water around unnecessarily. Lining the sack
with a water-tight stuff sack closed by a rubber band effectively
excludes water and also the damaging grit it carries with it. The
rope is both lighter and stronger for remaining dry, while
completely protected from any contamination. The sack is now also
bouyant and floats easily through any wet sections.

"SPECIAL PURPOSE" SACKS

Occasionally larger capacity sacks (Fig-24.) may be needed for the
deeper systems, while bivouacing underground, or when the
caving team is limited in number. Those sacks are essentially
similar to "Standard" tackle sacks, but are oval in shape with
carrying handles on the side and twin shoulder straps to enable
them to be worn on the back wherever the cave is large enough.
Such sacks are also useful on the surface for carrying equipment
to remote cave entrances, but are much less convenient in the
cave.

A rather more satisfactory solution for long surface marches;
where food and clothing may be needed along with caving
equipment, is the use of a large framed sack. This is more
comfortable; clothing and personal equipment are carried in the
sack itself (which is left at the cave entrance) with rope and
underground equipment packed in tackle sacks strapped on top.

2 – SINGLE ROPE TECHNIQUES

2 — SINGLE ROPE TECHNIQUES

2.1 DESCENT...............................27
General Considerations
Basic Manoeuvres
Descender - Loading and Use
Locking-Off
Intermediate Anchors
Descent/Ascent Changeovers
Passing a Knot
Tight Pitches
Bottom Belay

2.2 ASCENT................................34
Jammers - Characteristics
Climbing
Reverse Climbing
Intermediate Anchors
Passing a Knot
Ascent/Descent Changeover
Use of Safety-Cords
Muddy Ropes

2.3 SIGNALS 39
2.4 EFFICIENCY...........................39
Logistics
Progression with a Tackle Sack

2 — SINGLE ROPE TECHNIQUES

This section on single rope techniques, despite its length, describes little more than the basic skills needed to progress safely through the cave. These techniques are simple enough, but practical skills are not always readily learnt from written notes. By far the best way to learn is at first hand from an expert instructor, though tips from experienced cavers may also prove useful. The value of such techniques then lies in direct ratio to initial practice in a safe situation on the surface and subsequent experience gained gradually below ground. It is equally important to appreciate the particular hazards of the caving environment, especially in active systems, than become adept in SRT. The very nature of the activity determines that there is no substitute for experience, consequently these notes represent no more than a sound beginning.

2.1 DESCENT

Abseiling underground is an exhilarating experience. Unfortunately it is also one of the more hazardous aspects of these techniques. The disciplines involved are straightforward and relatively effortless in practice, although the grave inherent dangers are not always readily appreciated by those most at risk.

GENERAL CONSIDERATIONS

While descending a single fixed rope, the descender and the caver's hand beneath are the sole points of contact with the rope, and these are sliding rather than fixed contacts. Consequently, any loss of control or failure of the device tends to be serious. The caver effectively defies gravity. He does so by precisely varying the degree of friction between the rope and the descender from one moment to the next. For a given descender, the amount of friction depends on the type of rope, its condition (whether wet, dry or muddy), and the weight of the rope beneath, which decreases as the pitch is descended. The skill of the caver lies in compensating for these variables and effecting a smooth descent

such that he remains master of his own destiny. Familiarity
brings with it a tendency to descend too fast. This is easy to
understand, but is both completely pointless and very ill-advised.
The need is for precise control; once lost, even momentarily, it is
always difficult and sometimes impossible to regain. A smooth,
fully-controlled descent places the least amount of strain on the
descender, the rope system and the caver's nervous system.

While in mid-rope, the caver is in a very exposed position -
vulnerable to anchor, rope or equipment failure, water and
rockfall, loss of control, and a great many indignities arising from
carelessness. Amongst these are loose hair or clothing drawn into
the descender, tangles in the rope, or running out of rope before
the bottom of the pitch. Much of this is subjective, concentration
on the job and attention to detail will avoid most hazards, although
it may be mentioned in passing that even the most skilled caver
can be rendered inoperative by accident or injury and here lies
the intrinsic value of an auto-lock descending device.

In order to make life a little more secure, it is necessary to
carry prussiking gear on all descents. This makes it possible to
routinely pass knots, free trapped fingers and hair from the
descender, and to climb back up again should the situation either
prove too daunting or the rope too short. Descending a rope
without this facility for stopping at any point and immediately
climbing back up is only for the extremely stupid.

BASIC MANOEUVRES

The basic mid-rope manoeuvres listed here are few and simple,
nevertheless they are absolutely essential:

- Stop and securely lock-off the descender at
  any point during the descent
- Pass intermediate anchor points (rebelays).
- Change from descent to ascent and vice-versa.
- Pass knots in mid-rope.

DESCENDER - LOADING AND USE

The descender is attached by a screwgate karabiner or 10mm dia.
M/R to the central Delta M/R so that the pivoted side of the frame
is uppermost and the handle lies to the left. Locating the
descender at the highest point of the Delta M/R is necessary in
that it will inevitably slide to this position anyway when loaded,
possibly trapping other equipment fastened into the Delta.

Introducing the rope into the descender (Fig-25), there are two main points to remember in order to avoid loading it incorrectly.

1. The "live" (belayed) part of the rope always passes around the lower bollard first (the one closest to the caver).

2. The live rope enters from the left, the free section is then wound up between the bollards to emerge on the right.

Correct loading of the autolock descender. NOTE that threading this device wrongly, i.e. right to left, results in no autolock function.

Fig-25

The free rope is clipped into a braking karabiner which is aligned parallel and to the right of the long M/R, with the gate facing uppermost and the keeper pointing away, so that the rope is easily snapped into it. This karabiner, used to provide additional friction, should be of steel to avoid undue wear, and as there is no need of security, a snaplink is sufficient.

As the load is transferred to the descender, it can be seen that the lower eccentric bollard rotates a little and traps the rope. To control the descent, the right (controlling) hand grips the free rope so as to regulate its tension, while the left hand depresses the handle to release the auto-lock. It is important to realise that in common with any other descender, the descent is controlled mainly by tension in the lower rope. Squeezing the handle to release the auto-lock without this tension results in a fall. Managing both rope and descender takes a certain amount of skill and during initial practice the handle should be fully depressed and the descent controlled entirely by the rope slipping through the controlling hand, using the braking karabiner for additional friction. Later, with sufficient experience, it is possible to control the descent within very fine limits by balancing the amount the handle is depressed against tension from the controlling hand. It will be found, however, that too little tension provides an uncomfortably jerky descent and needlessly shock loads the rope, particularly when close to the belay. In this respect, the auto-lock function should be regarded as an additional option with little reliance placed on it, and certainly not as a substitute for direct control of the rope.

LOCKING-OFF

On some ropes the auto-lock may not function adequately and the descender creeps down the rope. Besides in any critical situation the descender must be locked-off manually.

The illustrations show three methods of locking-off the descender. In the first one, a "soft" lock (Fig-26), the rope is passed between the descender and the taut upper rope. This is sufficient to stop the descent should the auto-lock not grip, although the rope must still be held by the controlling hand.

The second method is a "hard" lock (Fig-27), where the left hand firmly grips the rope together with the descender above the handle, while a bight of rope is passed through the attachment karabiner or M/R and hooked over the descender. This is a safe method on a slack rope where the descender may possibly invert and cause a soft lock to release.

Fig-26 - Soft lock.

Fig-27 - Hard lock.

In any awkward location, the preferred method is a "full" lock (Fig-28), a combination of both soft and hard locks, also used to increase control where the auto-lock function of the descender has been deliberately made inoperative, in a tight pitch for example.

Fig-28 - Combination "Full" lock - essential with non-locking descenders.

Releasing any manual lock, the free part of the rope must remain firmly held in the controlling (right) hand while the other hand is used to undo the lock.

INTERMEDIATE ANCHORS (DESCENT)

Descend until level with the intermediate anchor (rebelay) and, if necessary, lock-off the descender. Clip the <u>short</u> safety-cord into the rope loop of the anchor, then continue descending a short way until the weight is taken entirely by the safety-cord (Fig-29). The descender is then transferred to the rope immediately below the anchor and locked-off securely (hard lock). In order to disconnect the safety-cord, the weight must be removed from it. Often there is a ledge or foothold that can be used momentarily. If not, place a knee or foot into the loop of rope coming from above and stand up in this (Fig-30). If all else fails, the lower rope can be wrapped around the boot a few times as a stirrup, or the climbing footloop clipped into the anchor. Having disconnected the safety-cord, unlock the descender and resume the descent.

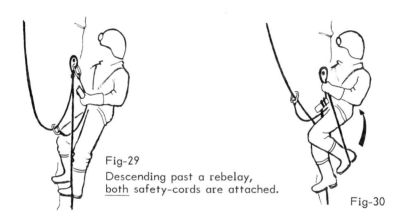

Fig-29
Descending past a rebelay,
<u>both</u> safety-cords are attached.

Fig-30

IMPORTANT

An additional precaution taken during training (and why not later?) is to clip the long safety-cord into the loop of slack rope at the rebelay during the manoeuvre (Fig-29) so that all is not lost should the descender be incorrectly loaded as the short safety-cord is released and the descender unlocked.

DESCENT/ASCENT CHANGEOVER

First stop and lock-off the descender (hard or full lock), then install the footloop jammer on the rope above. Stand up in this and with one arm crooked around the rope for balance, install the body-mounted jammer above the descender. This is easier if the jammer is opened in advance. Remove the descender from the rope and begin to climb.

32

PASSING A KNOT (DESCENT)

Should the rope prove too short, a further length can be added. Wherever possible, ropes should be joined at intermediate anchors to avoid the additional manoeuvres involved in passing the knot. Where this is not practical and the ropes are joined in mid-pitch, an extra "safety loop" is arranged at the joining knot (Fig-31). This is for the caver to attach himself to for extra security during the manoeuvre. In fact, this additional precaution is not strictly necessary during the descent as sufficient points of contact are maintained. However, it certainly does no harm to attach a safety-cord and takes but a moment.

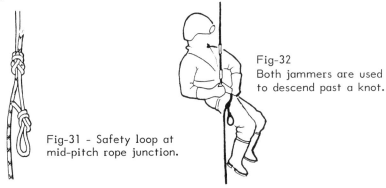

Fig-31 - Safety loop at mid-pitch rope junction.

Fig-32
Both jammers are used to descend past a knot.

Descend until the descender almost stops up against the joining knot (there is no need to lock-off), then install both jammers on the rope above, in effect changing to ascent (Fig-32). Transfer the descender to immediately below the knot and lock it off (hard lock). Now it is necessary to reverse the jammers down the half-metre or so of slack rope to a position immediately above the knot. Stand in the footloop, disconnect the body-mounted jammer and sit down onto the locked descender. It is worth noting that the tie-in cord linking the footloop jammer to the harness must be long enough not to become loaded at this point. Remove the footloop jammer (clip it to the harness), release the descender lock and resume the descent.

TIGHT PITCHES

In certain very narrow sections it may become difficult to operate the handle of an auto-lock descender, and the body of the device also tends to grind painfully into the ribs. A useful technique in these circumstances is to abseil with the descender attached to the short safety-cord at around shoulder level. This presents no particular difficulty, except that due care must be taken to prevent loose hair, beard, or helmet strap becoming trapped in the descender.

BOTTOM BELAY

During training, a descent can be protected to some extent by the technique of "bottom belay" (Fig-33). Someone holds the rope at the foot of the pitch in such a position that he can apply tension should the abseiler lose control. This has the effect of increasing friction around the descender, slowing or stopping the descent. Subsequently, the abseiler either resumes control or is lowered by the belayer. There are, however, certain disadvantages to this technique which preclude its use other than for training purposes. Increased safety for the abseiler is gained only at the expense of the belayer at the foot of the pitch. From this position he may have only limited visibility and insufficient time to react correctly. He is dangerously exposed to falling rocks, dropped equipment and perhaps a falling caver, any of which might injure or kill him. On a long pitch, even if sufficient warning is given, it is difficult because of the stretch in the rope to gain sufficient tension quickly enough. Where the rope is fastened to intermediate anchors in a pitch, this technique obviously can only be applied to the section of rope below the last rebelay.

NOTE that due to the reaction time and likely distraction of the belayer, apart from in very skilled hands, the protection afforded by this technique is largely illusory.

Fig-33 - Protecting a descent with a "bottom belay".

2.2 ASCENT

The technique used for climbing the rope is a straightforward "sit/stand" method widely known as the "Frog" technique. Two jammers are used, one body-mounted between the sit and chest-harnesses, the second higher up the rope carries the footloop. The climbing action is largely a matter of standing up and sitting down, with the arms used to lift the upper jammer and help stay upright.

In addition to climbing, the basic essential manoeuvres are:

- Reverse down the rope a short distance.

- Pass intermediate anchor points.

- Change from ascent to descent.

- Pass knots in mid-rope.

JAMMERS - CHARACTERISTICS

The two jammers most commonly used in these techniques (see p. 20) differ in shape but operate identically. To secure the cam in the open position in order to introduce the rope, the safety catch is pulled downwards and sideways against its spring and hooked over the frame (Fig-34). Once installed, the jammer slides upwards easily, but when pulled downward the cam acts to trap the rope against the frame and locks it firmly in place. The jammer cannot then be released until unloaded. Releasing or moving the jammer down the rope entails first lifting it fractionally to free the cam. Depressing the cam with a finger (in order to hold the teeth away from the rope) then allows the jammer to be lowered (Fig-35).

Fig-34
Safety catch in open position.

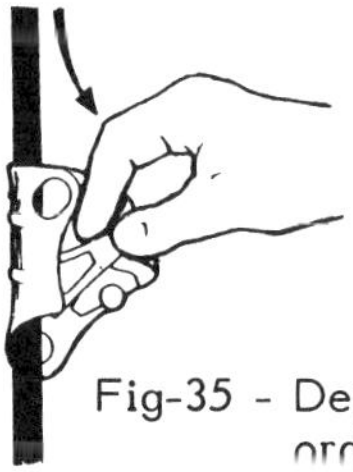

Fig-35 - Depressing the cam in order to lower a jammer.

The safety catch is fitted to the cam to prevent the jammer being removed from the rope accidently. This catch should <u>not</u> be used where the intention is only to slide the jammer down the rope. Removing the jammer from the rope involves first lifting it slightly to release the cam and then opening the safety catch to free the jammer completely.

Because the jammer must always be raised a little in order to free the cam, it follows that it should never be forced up against a knot in the rope. This effectively prevents it being lifted the small amount necessary and makes it impossible to remove - always stop a few centimetres short.

Given that jammers may only be released when unloaded and that while climbing each one is necessarily under load as the other is moved; it can be seen that provided both are attached to the harness, it is virtually impossible to fall from a free-hanging rope. Should the foot jammer fail, the climber sits supported by the body-mounted jammer, whilst failure of the body-mounted jammer results in a less comfortable hang from the cord connecting the foot jammer to his harness.

CLIMBING

Climbing is not difficult.

The footloop jammer is first installed on the rope and one foot placed in the loop. By standing in this the initial stretch is taken out of the rope before the body-mounted jammer is installed beneath. The caver's weight is then transferred to this supported by the sit-harness. With both hands clasped around the foot jammer (Fig-36), the knees are bent and raised as this is slid up the rope. Standing up in the footloop then automatically raises the body-mounted jammer (Fig-38).

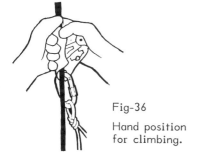

Fig-36

Hand position for climbing.

Fig-37

During the first few metres of climbing the rope has a tendency to ride up with the body-mounted jammer. This is overcome either by weighting the rope with a tackle sack or by trapping it between the boots (Fig-37). In the latter case, both feet are placed in the footloop with the rope between them. Holding the feet slightly apart as they are raised allows the rope to slip through, while standing up in the footloop brings them together, trapping the rope and pulling it through the jammer.

36

Climbing is easy but by no means effortless; raising 60-70kg? many metres up a rope requires a certain amount of work. It should be understood that the only muscles capable of repeatedly lifting bodyweight are those of the legs and buttocks. Furthermore, in order to climb vertically upwards maximum effort should be directed as near as possible straight down (Fig-38). Effort expended in any other direction, i.e. sideways, is less effective (Fig-39).

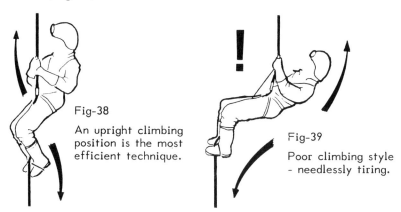

Fig-38

An upright climbing position is the most efficient technique.

Fig-39

Poor climbing style - needlessly tiring.

Efficient climbing involves developing a style of tucking the legs underneath and pulling into the rope with the arms in order to stay reasonably upright. The aim is to keep the upper body parallel and as close as possible to the rope. Wrapping the footloop around one leg helps a little but is rather less comfortable. The distance gained with each step varies with the climber but should be around 40-50cms. It is more economical to climb steadily than in short bursts. While it is possible to stop and rest at any time, frequent resting is generally a result of either climbing too fast, with poor style, or of course unfitness.

When climbing against a wall, one boot is placed in the footloop and the other used to fend off the rock, alternating legs occasionally to avoid fatigue. In a free-hanging pitch, both legs are used, either with both boots in the footloop, or one simply crossed on top of the other.

REVERSE CLIMBING

Reverse climbing is occasionally necessary to adjust position on the rope or to perhaps descend a loaded rope in an emergency. Essentially the exact opposite of climbing up, it is a matter of unloading the jammers before they can be moved down the rope. Stand up in the footloop, and with one arm crooked around the rope for balance, depress the cam of the body-mounted jammer with the other hand and move it down perhaps 30cms. Lower the foot jammer, and repeat the process as required. This manoeuvre is made easier if several short steps are taken rather than fewer longer ones. It is important to release the jammers only by depressing the cam without disengaging the safety catch.

INTERMEDIATE ANCHORS (ASCENT)

Climbing past an intermediate anchor (rebelay) presents no problem. Stop a few centimetres short of the belay knot and attach the long safety-cord to the anchor as a precaution. Stand in the footloop and transfer the body-mounted jammer to the upper rope (Fig-40) followed by the foot jammer. Progress a short distance, perhaps a metre, and once everything is working OK, unclip the safety-cord and continue up. At a rebelay it is almost always better to transfer the body-mounted jammer first, otherwise the elasticity of the rope above may make unloading this much more difficult.

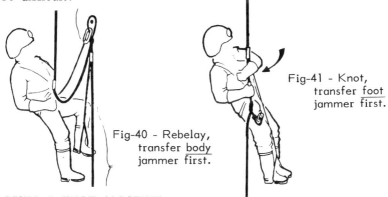

Fig-41 - Knot, transfer foot jammer first.

Fig-40 - Rebelay, transfer body jammer first.

PASSING A KNOT (ASCENT)

To pass a knot mid-rope, it is necessary to transfer the foot jammer first (it is, in fact, impossible to do otherwise). Stop just beneath the knot and clip a safety-cord into the loop provided for this purpose. Transfer the foot jammer to the rope above the knot and stand up in this with one arm around the rope for balance while transferring the body-mounted jammer (Fig-41). Disconnect the safety-cord and continue up.

ASCENT/DESCENT CHANGEOVER

To change from ascent to descent in mid-rope, first install the descender on the slack rope just beneath the body-mounted jammer and lock it off. Stand up in the footloop, disconnect the body-mounted jammer and sit back onto the descender. Note that the safety tie-in cord connecting the footloop jammer to the harness should be long enough not to become loaded at this point. Remove the foot jammer (clip it to the harness), unlock the descender and begin the descent.

USE OF SAFETY-CORDS

As a general rule, the fundamental principle of always maintaining a strong and secure connection with the rope implies a minimum of two points of contact. Note in particular that use of a single jammer has too low a safety margin. By continually bearing this in mind and attaching one or the other of the safety-cords whenever such a manoeuvre is required, the result should never prove disastrous even if a mistake is made. For example, as the top of the pitch is reached, a safety-cord is attached to the traverse line or main belay before any jammers are disconnected from the rope. Passing a tie-off point in the traverse line, one safety-cord is clipped onto the far side before the nearside one is removed (Fig-42). In short, the first action approaching an obstacle is to clip in a safety-cord and the last thing to do before moving off is to unclip it.

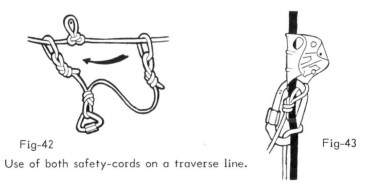

Fig-42   Fig-43

Use of both safety-cords on a traverse line.

MUDDY ROPES

A problem which may arise while climbing with sprung-cam jammers on a very muddy rope, is that mud compacted between the teeth of the cam causes the jammers to slip. In particularly muddy caves, it is better to use a lever-cam jammer (see p. 19) for the footloop, or at least carry a prussik-loop to provide a safe attachment while the jammer is removed from the rope and cleaned. A simple emergency measure used with a persistently slipping jammer is to wind the footloop around its attachment karabiner a couple of times (Fig-43) before carefully creeping up the rope!

2.3 SIGNALS

With the independence of movement characteristic of SRT, little communication between team members is necessary. The call "Rope free" (or a whistle signal) is used to indicate when an intermediate anchor has been passed – freeing a particular section of rope for the next climber or abseiler. "Below" is a warning call used in case of falling rock.

Generally during tackle hauling, or on wet (noisy) pitches where shouting may be misheard, three whistle signals are adopted.

> 1 blast = STOP
>
> 2 blasts = UP
>
> 3 blasts = DOWN

2.4 EFFICIENCY

Single rope techniques are by far the most efficient means of negotiating pitches, and the necessary equipment is comparatively compact and lightweight. Even so, caving is often strenuous; economy of movement through the cave is important and the efficient transport of equipment is directly related both to safety and to the enjoyment gained from a trip.

LOGISTICS

Small groups of 2, 3 or 4 cavers are the most efficient provided that they are not over-loaded with equipment. Each caver carries a sack containing his personal gear and his share of the rope and rigging equipment. Ropes are packed into sacks in the reverse order of use and the sacks numbered in the order they will be needed. During the descent, the team moves more or less together, so that minimum time is wasted either waiting for each other or for the correct equipment to arrive at the pitch. It is expedient to ensure that the appropriate sack is at the front of the team as each successive pitch is reached, tackle sacks show a remarkable tendency to gravitate towards the rear. Generally, the descent is relatively fast, the rate of progress largely determined by the time taken rigging.

On the return, the time taken to climb the pitches has rather more effect, but whether a particular pitch takes 10 or 15 minutes to climb is of little consequence. Far more important is the overall competence of the team moving through the cave and the avoidance of unnecessary delays. Where a pitch is rigged with intermediate anchors, each caver signals as the rebelay is passed so that the next caver can begin to climb the rope. Thus in order to save time a number of cavers can climb simultaneously provided they are each hanging from a separate belay. There is no reason to wait at the top of each pitch until the whole team is up, this would result in a "log jam" and an unnecessary delay at the next pitch. Better if each caver moves more or less independently, perhaps in pairs, provided that each carries his share of the equipment.

PROGRESSION WITH A TACKLE SACK

Each individual caver carrying a share of the rigging equipment and making his own way through the cave is a fundamental aspect of modern caving technique. Long gone are the days of passing tackle from hand to hand along crawls or traverses, huge mounds of gear at the foot of each pitch, and interminable waits sat around shivering until the stuff was eventually dragged up.

With SRT, a caver's sack will generally contain his personal equipment which must always be with him, together with any emergency equipment he might carry. In a cave where the rope is rebelayed in a pitch, lowering or hauling is not possible without extra ropes and the sack must be carried anyhow. The sack is fastened to the caver's waistbelt or to the Delta M/R of his harness by a cord, which might equally well be permanently attached to the sack or a separate length of light rope.

In large passages the sack is slung from the shoulder/s, or carried by hand using the central grip handle where it is necessary to stoop. For sideways progress along narrow canyon passages, the sack is held in the trailing hand by an upper handle or the hauling loops, or alternatively hung directly from the waistbelt on the same side.

Fig-44

Fig-45

In a straightforward crawl the sack is simply dragged along by its cord guided where necessary by the feet. In more tortuous crawlways where jamming is likely it may be better to push the sack on ahead (Fig-44). Here the sack must of course be smaller than the passage! In a particularly tight system a long, thin sack is useful. When climbing or traversing, the sack is often left to dangle between the legs on its cord (Fig-45).

The principle of "carrying your own sack" as an essential part of caving technique is particularly relevant to the vertical bits. Here the sack is suspended from the belt (Fig-46) or on its cord, so when abseiling the weight is in fact supported by the descender and hardly noticed. For the ascent, a similar technique is used, the length of cord such that the sack either dangles just beneath the feet, which avoids standing on it, or is clipped directly to the main harness attachment which prevents it swinging about and twisting around the rope (Fig-47). Here, with heavier loads, sit/stand climbing rigs have the advantage that both legs work together during each lift, and for much of the climbing cycle the load is supported by the body-mounted jammer (Fig-48).

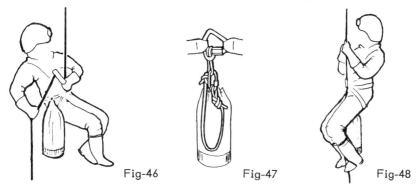

Fig-46   Fig-47   Fig-48

In water-filled passages, the sack is simply floated behind, although care must be taken to ensure that the sack is buoyant wherever swimming is necessary. An inner "stuff sack" of waterproof fabric or an ordinary polythene bag closed by a rubber band will make the sack buoyant and also keep the contents dry.

Fig-49 - Separate watertight stuff sack used as liner in tackle sack.

EQUIPMENT CHECKLIST

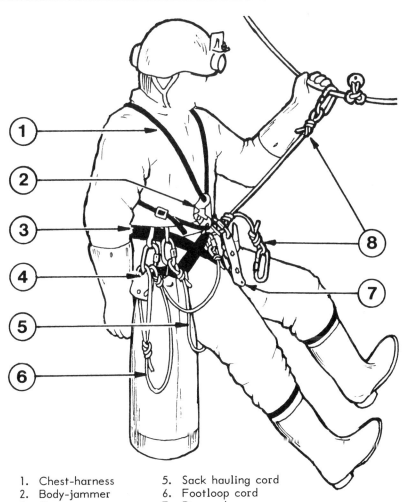

1. Chest-harness
2. Body-jammer
3. Sit-harness
4. Footloop jammer
5. Sack hauling cord
6. Footloop cord
7. Descender
8. Safety-cords

3 – RIGGING EQUIPMENT

3 — RIGGING EQUIPMENT

3.1 ROPE 45
Basic Materials
Construction
Rope Size
Rope Strength
Tensile Strength
Energy Absorption
Static Stretch
Abrasion Resistance
Heat Resistance
Chemical Damage
Sunlight

3.2 ROPE CARE 50
New Rope
Marking Ropes
Rope Transport
Washing and Inspection
Storage
Rope Life
Drop Test

3.3 BOLT ANCHORS 55
Anchor Sleeves
Bolts

3.4 HANGERS 56
Function
Plate Hangers
Self-Contained Hangers

3.5 BOLT KIT...............................58

3 — RIGGING EQUIPMENT

3.1 ROPE

The rope is the single most important element in the SRT system. Its selection and subsequent use are vital matters of life and death. Modern caving (speleo) ropes are meticulously designed pieces of equipment, possessing quite remarkable properties; used correctly they are perfectly safe. The situation is complicated, however, by ropes of roughly similar appearance having varying properties built into them which may make them more suitable for one purpose than another, high and low stretch for example. It is therefore necessary to understand a little of the properties and capabilities of a rope in order to choose the right type and to be able to use it safely and effectively.

BASIC MATERIALS

Currently there are but two common fibres suitable for speleo ropes, Polyamide (Nylon) and Polyester (Terylene). Both these fibres are virtually identical in appearance and roughly equivalent in terms of tensile strength, although each has particular advantages and disadvantages in certain applications. Polyamide, for instance is an inherently stretchy fibre used to great advantage in very extensible climbing ropes which are required to absorb considerable amounts of energy in arresting falls. Polyester fibres have much less inherent stretch which simplifies the construction of a low stretch speleo rope, but also markedly lessens its capacity to absorb a shock or "dynamic" load. Although virtually all modern caving ropes are of Nylon, it is nevertheless possible to construct a low stretch rope from either Nylon or Terylene and the relative importance of this particular factor is considered later.

CONSTRUCTION

Current speleo ropes are almost exclusively of a "kernmantle" (i.e. sheath and core) type of construction (Fig-50), comprising a "core" of more or less parallel bunches of fibres accounting for perhaps 70% of the mass of the rope, contained in a tightly woven "sheath" which holds the core together and protects it from damage. The caver effectively climbs up the sheath, so this must be adequately strong and preferably constructed so as not to slide down the core should the sheath itself be severed. Sheath and core are, however, joined together whenever the rope is knotted. The core is the main load-bearing member, determining both the overall breaking load of the rope, the amount it stretches, and consequently its capacity to absorb shock-loads.

Fig-50 - Kernmantel Construction. The basis of most current SRT ropes.

ROPE SIZE

An appropriate size of rope for these techniques is around 10mm dia. A thicker rope would be stronger but also heavier and more bulky. The thinnest rope of any real use is about 9mm dia., with current technology, it is impractical to build sufficient strength and energy absorption into a thinner rope. The optimum size of 10mm dia. is also directly related to its mass. A thin rope, although perhaps strong enough, has a proportionately greater surface area and, of course, fewer fibres than a thicker rope. Consequently, it is far more vulnerable to weakening from general deterioration and significant abrasion damage due to losses from severed fibres.

ROPE STRENGTH

The effective "strength" of a rope comprises two main factors: its "tensile" breaking load and its capacity to absorb a "dynamic" shock load Both these factors are compromised to some extent in a speleo rope, but it is far more important that the rope be capable of absorbing the dynamic loads resulting from a fall than for it to have a very high breaking load.

TENSILE STRENGTH

Consider first the tensile strength, which is the figure quoted on a reel of rope. A figure of around 2000kg is adequate for a new rope, but don't be misled by this "tensile breaking load": it's a figure arrived at in a laboratory with little practical value. Tests have shown that the breaking load of a rope may be halved simply by knotting and further drastically reduced after only moderate use underground. The effective strength of a used rope, one that is neither badly worn nor damaged, is in fact very different from the tensile strength quoted by the manufacturer. The overall picture is a complex one, but while this residual degree of strength is adequate in normal use there remains only a relatively small safety margin. Consequently any further weakening, such as damage to the rope arising from abrasion against the rock, must be avoided at all costs.

ENERGY ABSORPTION

The capacity of a rope to absorb a shock-load depends on how much it stretches. This is important, if for example, a caver were to fall a certain distance attached to a slack rope which then suddenly becomes taut. A stretchy rope slows and stops the fall relatively gently, while a low-stretch rope causes an abrupt halt. The less stretch, the higher the dynamic loading or "impact force". The greater the stretch, the lower the impact force, as energy is more effectively absorbed by the rope. The "peak impact force" then is the maximum energy developed in the rope arresting a fall. This is transmitted along the rope to the caver at one end and the belay at the other. Clearly it is vital that the rope has a certain amount of stretch, otherwise following a severe fall the resultant force will either break the rope, destroy the belay, or damage the caver.

Unlike tensile tests in a laboratory, in a cave the only loads that are likely to threaten the rope's integrity are generated by falls. The magnitude of such loads is largely determined by the "fall-factor".

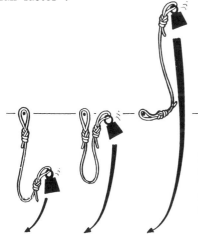

Fig-51 - Fall Factor - A theoretical relationship between the length of fall and amount of rope available to absorb the shock-load produced in arresting it.

FF 0.5   FF 1.0   FF 2.0

The term fall-factor describes the relationship between the length of a fall and the length of rope available to intercept it. Understand first that whilst the energy developed in a fall is proportional to the distance fallen, a rope's capacity to absorb this energy is proportional to its length. By dividing one by the other (i.e. length of fall divided by length of free rope) the result is a fall-factor which varies between 0 and 2. The tricky bit is that, apart from very small falls, it is the relationship between these two factors which is important rather than their value. Which simply means, for example, that in the case of a factor-1 fall (where the fall and the length of rope are equal) a 2m fall onto 2m of rope in general produces the same shock-load (impact force) as a 10m fall onto 10m of rope (Fig-51).

Because speleo ropes are low stretch, and accordingly have only a limited capacity to absorb energy, they must never be subject to a situation where a high factor fall is possible. A factor-1 fall with a load of 80kg may produce an impact force approaching 700kg (more correctly 7,000 Newtons, see   ) which is uncomfortably close to both the limitations of the equipment and the force a caver might withstand without sustaining severe injury.

"STATIC" STRETCH

An ideal speleo rope would be relatively inelastic at low levels, say up to 200kg or so (a typical value for someone climbing the rope rather energetically) and increasingly elastic at higher loads. This would avoid unpleasant bouncing in the rope on long pitches and minimise dangerous reciprocation against the rock, but retain the shock-absorbency needed to safely arrest a small fall. Current speleo ropes are compromised in this respect; with a typical value of perhaps 2-3% stretch under a load of 80kg and 30-40% elongation at breaking load - compared with around 8% and 60% respectively for a climbing rope.

ABRASION RESISTANCE

To some extent abrasion resistance is an important factor in a speleo rope. Apart from ageing it is probably this that determines its useful life. However, with regard to rubbing against rock, NO rope is adequately abrasion resistant. The concept of poor rigging being safe because a particular rope is said to have "good abrasion resistance" is a completely misguided one - it most certainly has not. Limestone is harder than rope and any rope rubbing over rock will abrade. The only sensible solution is to avoid this type of abrasion altogether by meticulous rigging. Ropes are only completely safe rigged clear of the rock.

Apart from surface abrasion of the sheath, which is more or less obvious, a rope will abrade internally in use due to particles of silt trapped within the fibres. This drastically weakens the rope which is why thorough washing is important.

HEAT RESISTANCE

Rope materials suffer a decrease in strength with an increase in temperature, weakening markedly above 150°C and melting at around 250°C. Since all descenders necessarily utilise friction, they all get hot to some extent. Fortunately temperatures high enough to damage rope significantly are beyond the bounds of normal safe technique. Considering that metal devices become too hot to hold at around 65°C and that ropes are more often wet than not, this is a factor of relatively minor importance. Nevertheless descenders with steel surfaces in contact with the rope (steel has a much lower thermal conductivity than aluminium) readily become locally hot enough to fuse the outer fibres of a dry rope. This stiffens the surface of the rope, making it hard and unpleasant to handle. Such damage is easily avoided, just descend at a sensible rate and on a long, dry pitch, wet the rope first.

CHEMICAL DAMAGE

While both Polyester and Polyamide are extremely stable polymers affected by comparatively few common chemicals, it is well known that Polyamide (Nylon) is severely affected by quite dilute acids, and Polyester (Terylene) is most readily attacked by strong alkalies. The most likely source of these contaminants is leaky mining lamp batteries, although there are of course others. In both these cases irreversible damage takes place within a matter of minutes, so subsequent washing is not an answer. There is no solution to the insidious hazard of chemical damage other than by avoiding any possible contamination altogether. The first step in this regard is to use a proper lamp.

SUNLIGHT

All synthetic rope materials are degraded to some extent by sunlight, or more specifically, by ultra-violet light. To what extent a certain rope is affected over a given period is difficult to quantify, but it will certainly not be affected by sunlight in the dark. So a rope in regular use underground, carried in a tackle sack, and stored in a cellar, will be least affected. It is also apparent that only the surface fibres of the rope are exposed, which contribute comparatively little to its strength and which

hopefully serve to protect the fibres beneath, so that any
weakening should be marginal. In the absence of any reliable
hard figures however, it makes good sense to dry and store ropes
in the shade rather than find out the hard way.

3.2 ROPE CARE

On each pitch the caver depends entirely on a single rope; the
care and protection of this rope is vital to his continued existence
and demands rather more attention in both these respects than is
commonly realised in practice. Neglect the rope at your peril. It
is just as important to use and care for ropes properly as to select
a suitable rope in the first place.

NEW ROPES

A new rope should be washed before use. This removes the
lubricants used in manufacture and also shrinks the rope – which
serves both to compact the sheath and tighten it onto the core –
improving its wearing properties.

Soak the rope overnight in clean water, drain and then remove
surplus water by pulling the rope through an anchored descender.
Repeat the process two more times, pulling the rope through the
descender in the same direction, then hang it up to dry. Later,
cut off any surplus sheath that has crept along the rope and melt
the ends to prevent unravelling. This procedure will help prevent
sheath slippage during the initial few trips until the sheath is
properly bedded.

When first washed, all ropes (particularly Nylon ones) shrink
by varying amounts up to about 10%. It is as well to more or less
determine this amount before cutting and marking ropes for
length. However, the rope will continue to shrink, albeit at a
much lower rate, throughout its life and it's unwise to place too
much reliance on the exact length marked. New ropes are better
in longer lengths. Later they can be cut, perhaps at a damaged
section, into shorter lengths.

MARKING ROPES

As a minimum, ropes should be marked to indicate length, type
(static or dynamic), and age. There are many ways of doing this,
the main criteria being durability and that the information is clear
and legible.

Generally, information is better written than coded (without the key a code is meaningless). A simple method is to bind the rope about 5cms from the end with a couple of turns of PVC adhesive tape. The information is written on this with waterproof (ball point pen) ink, e.g. ST-30, 5/86 (30m static rope dating from May 1986) and then protected by two coats of some clear plastic adhesive. This method of marking, though crude, remains legible for a considerable period and can easily be renewed. A rather more sophisticated method is to bind the end with PVC tape, then adhesive figures such as those used by electricians for marking cables, held in place by clear PVC heat-shrink sleeving.

Fig-52 - Rope marked indicating
owner, type, length & age.

However, do not bind the end of a rope in a way that increases its diameter significantly, nor makes more than a few centimetres rigid and prone to getting caught up.

ROPE TRANSPORT

Ropes should always be carried underground in a tackle sack. These are far easier to handle than coiled ropes and protect the rope very effectively from damage while being transported through the cave. It certainly makes better sense to wear out the sack rather than the rope. Lining the sack with a watertight stuff sack closed by a rubber band will also exclude water and the damaging grit it carries with it (see Fig-49). The rope is both lighter and stronger for remaining dry. Should a rope get dirty on the way to a pitch, the silt is then forcibly ground into the body of the rope while it is being used. This rapidly wears out metal equipment and rope alike while making it impossible to subsequently remove all the silt from the rope.

WASHING AND INSPECTION

After each trip, ropes should be washed and inspected for wear or damage. Thorough washing is important to remove as much as possible of the silt particles which act to abrade the subsurface fibres of the rope and weaken it as well as making it stiff.

Superficial mud can be removed simply by sloshing the rope around in running water, perhaps a stream by the cave. This is rarely sufficient however, and more stubborn dirt might call for soaking and then pulling a few times through a simple rope-washer until the water runs clear (Fig-53).

After washing, ropes must be carefully inspected for signs of damage or excessive wear. The method is to run the rope through the hands a few centimetres at a time, flexing it and feeling for any soft spots or regions of reduced diameter as well as the more obvious flaws. Where necessary, the rope should be cut at the damaged section and re-marked before being stored. There is no particular merit in drying a rope before storing it. Ropes are not harmed if left to dry slowly until the next trip.

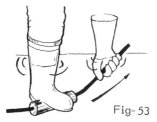

Rope washer - The rope is fed through a pad of bristles in a plastic tube. The washer is held underwater and the rope pulled to and fro until clean.

Fig-53

STORAGE

Ropes are best kept in a cool, dark, well-ventilated place, loosely coiled and hung on either plastic tubes, untreated wooden pegs or rope loops (Fig-54). Given that ropes used underground are generally fed loose into a sack and only coiled for storage, it makes no sense to adopt a method of coiling which creates twists in the rope, which must later be untwisted as the rope is packed. This is the case with the normal mountaineering method of coiling rope. A simple, more practical method is to form the rope into hanks by laying loops across one hand, subsequently secured with a few turns of rope (Fig-55). Handling long lengths of rope, this process is speeded up and made easier by wrapping the rope around three sturdy pegs fixed into a wall (Fig-56).

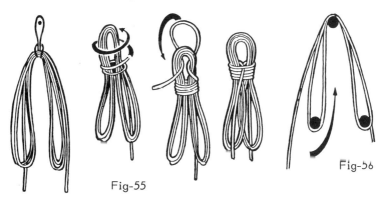

Fig-54   Fig-55   Fig-56   Method of Coiling Ropes.

The diagram (Fig-57) shows a simple, free-standing rope rack, easily made and providing storage space for many hundreds of metres of rope. In a well-lit location, the rack can be covered with a tarpaulin.

Fig-57 - Rope storage rack. Best located in a cool, dark, well ventilated place. Away from any hazardous chemicals.

WARNING

Anyone finding that they are just too busy (or lazy) for this amount of routine maintenance is definitely in the wrong game. A caver's life depends totally on his rope; much better to give up caving altogether than kill himself by neglect of his equipment.

ROPE LIFE

There is no practical method of determining exactly the safe life of a rope, dependent as it is on matters of age, care and usage. Nothing short of a test to destruction reveals the true condition of a rope and consequently ropes must either be tested or discarded arbitrarily on grounds of obvious wear, damage, or age.

As in all considerations related to safety, the decision to retire a rope should err (if at all) on the side of survival. A fairly new sheathed rope can probably be used relatively safely until the sheath is very worn, although when the sheath no longer effectively protects the core - throw it out. This crude method, of course, takes no account of the weakening effects of age or general deterioration due to other factors - in fact, the appearance of a rope doesn't reveal much at all.

DROP TEST

A far more precise indication of a rope's condition is gained by subjecting a short section of it to a destructive drop test. A drop test rig is used to apply two consecutive shock-loads resulting

54

from a factor-1 fall with an 80kg mass. If a rope can withstand this, it is considered adequate (Fig-58).

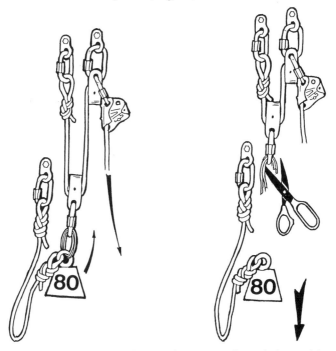

Fig-58 - Drop Test Rig. The weight is raised until the end knots in the rope sample are level (i.e. FF 1.0) and the loops of cord cut (from a safe distance with a knife fixed at the end of a stick).

The tests are made on 2m samples cut from the rope, a Fig-8 Knot is tied in each end to provide a test piece about 1m long, and the samples soaked in water overnight. Should the rope support only one shock and break on the second one, then the test must be repeated with a further sample from the same rope. If it again supports a single shock then the rope is adequate, but should be tested again before too long.

It is recommended that ropes are tested routinely after three year's regular use and annually thereafter. Regardless of age, any rope about which there is doubt should be tested immediately.

Speleo ropes are relatively expensive in the quantities required, and although this is a good reason for carefully avoiding damage, it's no reason at all for continuing to use a suspect rope. Either get it tested or relegate it to the club dig.

3.3 BOLT ANCHORS

The type of anchor adopted by cavers throughout Europe for rigging ropes is a "self-drilling" anchor sleeve (brand name "SPIT"), which is first used to drill the fixing hole and then permanently embedded in the rock (Fig-59). It accepts an 8mm dia. fixing bolt securing a hanger to which the rope is attached (see Fig-68).

Fig-59   Fig-60

ANCHOR SLEEVES

Self-drilling anchor sleeves are made from case-hardened tubular steel, plated to resist corrosion, with cutting teeth at one end and an 8mm dia. thread at the other. The toothed end of the anchor has grooves machined along part of its length, intended to split and allow expansion when a conical wedge is forcibly inserted, thereby gripping the sides of the fixing hole.

BOLTS

The fixing bolts most generally used are 8mm dia. ISO-metric hexagon headed set-screws, requiring a 13mm spanner (Fig-60). Such bolts should be forged from high-tensile steel of at least 8.8 spec (marked on the head of the bolt), which indicates a theoretical maximum breaking load of about 1800kg. However, a bolt breaks when the total load applied to it (that is the load on the rope plus the tightening force on the bolt) exceeds this figure. So overtightening the bolt serves only to reduce the load it can support. Fingertight plus an additional half-turn with a spanner is sufficient; deliberately shortening spanners in order to reduce leverage is a very good idea.

A significant recent development is the use of socket-headed cap bolts and an Allen Key type hex-wrench (Fig-61/2). These bolts are available in very high quality steel (12.9 spec) and the 6mm wrench is both lighter than a spanner and avoids any possibility of overtightening

Fig-61   Fig-62

3.4 HANGERS

FUNCTION

Hangers provide the means of attaching the rope to the fixed anchor. Basically, the function of a hanger is to transmit the load on the rope via the anchor to the surrounding rock without excessively stressing either the anchor or the fixing bolt. This in practice means that the belay is often load in "shear" (more or less perpendicular to the bolt) and that the hanger design must ensure any leverage or bending action on the bolt is minimised.

Hangers fall into two broad categories: those which require a karabiner to attach the rope and those which do not.

PLATE HANGERS

These generally consist of a bent or twisted plate with holes for a bolt and a karabiner. Shapes vary considerably, but there are two main configurations, one where the karabiner rests perpendicular to the rock surface (Fig-63), and one where it lies more or less parallel to it (Fig-64). The difference is important – hangers positioning the karabiners at right angles are primarily designed for use with an oval karabiner which rests against the rock and helps support the load. This is occasionally advantageous against a vertical wall in that it positions the rope a little away from the rock and helps prevent the knot abrading.

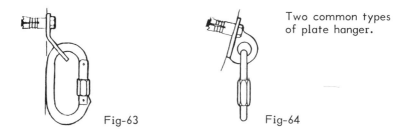

Two common types of plate hanger.

Fig-63   Fig-64

Somewhat more versatile is the type of hanger where the karabiner lies parallel to the rock (particularly those designed to accept two karabiners), although such hangers do require careful positioning to avoid abrasion of the attached knot. All the hangers in this first category (plate hangers) suffer from similar disadvantages in that a karabiner is required to attach the rope, that incorrect positioning can cause dangerous leverage to both hanger and bolt, and that substantial "dressing" of the rock may be necessary for the hanger to sit correctly.

In many cases, Maillon Rapides are a preferred alternative to karabiners with such hangers, being lighter, more secure and avoiding the potential weakness of a hinged gate (Fig-65). With this in mind, karabiners are best positioned with the keeper pointing downwards, so that gravity ensures the sleeve remains screwed up (Fig-66). Contrary to general opinion, loading the rope over the reduced diameter of the M/R, provided this is of 7mm dia. or greater, does not weaken the attachment significantly as the rope will always suffer greater distortion within the knot.

7mm Ø Long Series Maillon Rapide used for attachment to a plate hanger.

Fig-65

Karabiner arranged with keeper pointing down and gate facing out from wall.

Fig-66

SELF-CONTAINED HANGERS

Superior in many respects are hangers which do not require a karabiner, where the rope is fixed directly to the hanger. Again there are two types: "Ring-hangers", solid metal loops which protrude at right angles to the rock (Fig-67), and a more recent design, "Bollards", where the rope rests more or less directly on the bolt (Fig-68).

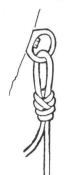

Bollard Hanger - The rope rests directly on the bolt eliminating any unwanted leverage from the hanger.

Ring Hanger - tied directly into the rope.

Fig-67

Fig-68

Ring-hangers are a multi-purpose hanger knotted directly onto the rope and most advantageous where the load is applied at a considerable angle to the rock. It is vital, however, to ensure that the ring is orientated along the same plane as the rope in order to avoid dangerous bending moments in the bolt. An offset or D-shaped rather than a circular ring also minimises leverage on the bolt when the load is applied at a close angle to the rock.

58

With the Bollard hangers, the rope is fastened directly around the bolt and held in position by a captive washer or "cage". The rope is trapped firmly against the rock eliminating abrasion at this point and ensuring that the load is transferred to the anchor with minimal leverage on the bolt.

These systems have certain advantages:

- Substantial weight savings - no karabiners.
- The direction of applied load is rather less critical.
- Often the strength of the anchor is substantially increased.
- Elimination of a potential weak point in the karabiner gate.

Given adequate strength, the most important single factor relating a suitable hanger to a particular situation is the priority of protecting the rope from abrasion damage. This determines that the best location for an anchor is in somewhat overhanging rock, so that the rope hangs clear or alternatively is directed away from the rock by the configuration of the belay (Fig-69).

The optimum loading angle for most types of hanger is at a slight angle to the vertical (assuming a horizontal anchor). A factor common to all hangers (apart from Ring-hangers) is that the load should not be directed at an angle greater than about 45° to the rock surface (Fig-69).

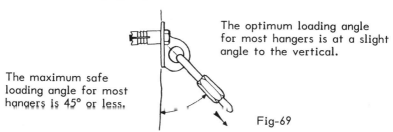

The maximum safe loading angle for most hangers is 45° or less.

The optimum loading angle for most hangers is at a slight angle to the vertical.

Fig-69

It is important that hangers are firmly bolted to the anchor so that they cannot be accidently inverted or the bolt work itself loose. However, overtightening a bolt serves only to reduce the load it can support, fingertight plus an additional half-turn with a spanner is sufficient.

3.5 BOLT KIT

Underground the necessary tools and accessories for installing bolt anchors are best carried as a self-contained kit, with the individual components arranged conveniently to hand and so as to minimise accidental loss.

The basic tools are a hammer, an anchor-driver and a spanner or hex-wrench. The accessories consist of self-drilling Spit anchors and expansion wedges, hangers with integral bolts and, if necessary, karabiners or M/Rs for attaching the rope. Useful additions are a plastic "blow tube" for clearing spoil from the hole during drilling, a makeshift tool for removing wet or compacted rock dust from the anchor sleeve, and a small container of grease.

Fig-70 - Bolting Kit.

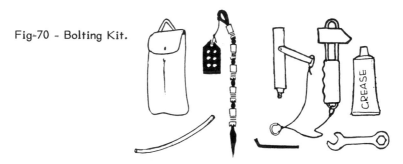

The illustration (Fig-70) shows the layout of such a kit carried in a small pouch. Both hammer and driver are connected to a small karabiner by a length of cord and clipped to the pouch. In use, this karabiner is attached to some convenient point (chest-strap?) to avoid any possibility of dropping the tools down the pitch. The spanner or hex-wrench is also fitted with a cord attached to the harness or, as some cavers prefer, to a rubber band worn on the upper arm. Anchor sleeves are carried slipped onto a 10mm wide strip of inner tube (tapered at the end) and expansion wedges pressed into a 20mm thick pad of closed-cell foam with suitable holes punched in it, both fixed directly to the inside of the pouch.

NOTE

Caving equipment is subject to harsh use under far from ideal conditions, but is designed to require only the minimum of maintenance All that any of this equipment really needs to keep it in working order is washing and drying; this takes very little time and should not be neglected.

FURTHER TRAINING

This book is not a comprehensive manual of vertical caving techniques, but one of a series of practical handbooks intended for the fairly experienced caver interested in developing his technical skills. The techniques described here are limited to those concerned with safe, routine progress through the cave. More advanced techniques and the essential skills of self-help rescue are the subject of a separate book.

There can be no doubt about the value of specialised training to the caver eager to learn his craft, but equally there is no substitute for practical experience and no short cut to gaining it. Becoming a safe, competent caver is a gradual process where familiarity with the techniques of progression is really only a starting point.

Ultimately the satisfaction realised in overcoming the obstacles which exist underground depends not on taking foolish risks and hoping for the best, but in clear-headed judgment and experience at matching dangers with the appropriate skills. Compared with many so-called "risk activities" caving is a reasonably safe pursuit. However, it is intrinsic in the very nature of the activity that cavers be effectively independent and capable of dealing with the problems that inevitably arise from time to time. Accident or injury may place any caver in the situation where he is dependent on help from his colleagues. Consequently, it is vital that all cavers be proficient in first aid and self-help rescue procedures and so able to offer effective help in an emergency.

4 – EXPLORATION TECHNIQUES

4 — EXPLORATION TECHNIQUES

4.1 ANCHORS 63
Natural Anchors
Bolt Anchors
S/D Anchor Placement
Marking Anchors
Maintenance

4.2 KNOTS 67
General Points
Types - Applications
Loop Knots
Joining Knots
Safety Loop
Back-up Knots

4.3 PACKING ROPES 71
Surface
Underground
Coiling Ropes

4.4 RIGGING 73
General Considerations
Traverse Line
Main Anchor
Double Anchors
Bolt Hangers
Intermediate Anchors
Joining Ropes

4.5 SUPPLEMENTARY TECHNIQUES...80
Cable Tethers
Rope Protectors
Deviation
Pendulums
Avoiding Shock-Loads
Shock Absorption Knots

4.6 WET PITCHES 85
Hazards
Special Techniques

4.7 DE-RIGGING 87
Hauling

4 — EXPLORATION TECHNIQUES

4.1 ANCHORS

Modern techniques of rigging ropes in caves and the implicit need to avoid rope abrasion demands that strong anchor points are available exactly where they are required. Occasionally, natural rock features may provide suitable anchors, or cracks where chocks or pitons may be placed, but for the most part these techniques dictate the use of bolt anchors. Natural anchors are but rarely located in a position providing a suitable hang for the rope and are used mainly as back-up anchors or for the traverse line, where exact positioning is less critical.

NATURAL ANCHORS

The rock features suitable for use as anchors are more or less obvious and often the rope is tied directly around such anchors in order to avoid the extra equipment and potential weak links introduced by a karabiner and sling. Sharp edges which might damage the rope can be felt for and rounded off with a hammer, or padded with a tackle sack. Occasionally a sling is used to prevent undue wear to the main rope or to save rope; for this purpose 3m circumference slings tied from 8/9mm dia. rope are both strong and durable (Fig-71).

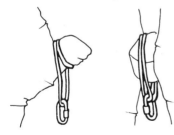

Fig-71 - 8mm Ø rope slings prevent wear, save rope and are easily replaced when worn.

The strength of a natural anchor is always indeterminate and care must be taken to check that the rock is sound. Striking with a hammer should produce a clear, ringing note. If it produces a dull, hollow sound the anchor may be flawed or insecurely planted and should not be trusted.

BOLT ANCHORS

Natural anchors are useful for fixing traverse lines but, it is almost always necessary to rig the rope in the pitch from bolts. In a cave that has been descended a number of times, the bolt anchors may be found in place in the rock and simply require checking and hangers bolting to them. Often it is difficult to determine exactly where the rope should hang without first descending the pitch. In situ anchors may be extremely inconspicuous and some diligence is required to ensure that these are not overlooked. Otherwise it is necessary to install whatever 8mm anchors are required in order to rig the rope safely, but not without considerable attention both to precise location and correct placement.

Installing bolt hangers underground raises certain ethical questions which place a degree of responsibility on the cavers whose techniques require them. Such anchors form the basis of current techniques of rigging rope and we must take care not to lose touch with reality: Safety rules O/K - if a bolt anchor is clearly necessary then it should (and doubtless will) be placed. But the burden of this statement is that increasing numbers of bolt anchors are placed in a thoughtless fashion in silly locations without due regard to technical considerations let alone ethics. Is it too much to expect cavers to justify their actions, to consider each situation carefully and make an intelligent decision on whether to place a bolt or not?

Where anchors are placed they must be properly installed, a simple enough procedure and a fundamental part of the caver's craft, but rarely the case to judge from the sorry examples left sticking out of cave walls. Furthermore, is it not for all cavers using these anchors to ensure they are maintained in a safe condition for as long as possible?

S/D ANCHOR PLACEMENT

Select an area of sound rock free from any fissures or veins of softer material, an anchor cannot withstand a higher load than the rock surrounding it. By chipping with the hammer, clean the immediate area of any corroded surface rock or irregularities, so that the anchor is placed entirely in sound rock and the attached hanger will lie flat against the rock surface. It is important to drill at right angles to this surface (Fig-72), so that the anchor is completely supported by the surrounding rock and to ensure that the hanger stresses neither anchor nor bolt unnecessarily.

The fixing hole is made by fitting the anchor to an adaptor tool (driver) and using this as a percussion drill. By repeated sharp blows with a light hammer while the driver is rotated to and fro, the cutting teeth bite at a slightly different place each time and the hole is progressively deepened. It is necessary to remove the drill from the hole frequently to clear the powdered rock, by tapping it out of the anchor and blowing the hole clear by means of a short length of plastic tubing. It takes between 10 and 20 minutes to drill the hole depending on its location and the nature of the rock. The first few millimetres of drilling are the most critical, care being needed to keep the cutting teeth in exactly the same position until the hole is deep enough to guide the drill – about 5mm. Continue drilling until the full length of the anchor sleeve is sunk below the surface of sound rock by about 3mm, then remove and clear both the anchor sleeve and the hole completely of any spoil. Lightly press the conical expansion wedge into the end of the anchor and replace it in the hole, then without rotating the driver, hammer the anchor home until it is flush or slightly beneath the rock surface. This has the effect of forcing the cone into the anchor causing it to expand and grip the sides of the hole (Fig-73). Unscrew the driver, re-check the anchor and surrounding rock for flaws, insert a little grease to help combat corrosion and fit the bolt and hanger.

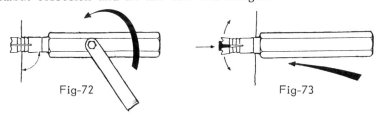

Fig-72   Fig-73

A few general points – it is important that the hole is drilled deep enough that the anchor does not protrude unsupported from the rock (Fig-74). To be hard enough for drilling, the anchor sleeve is extremely brittle and may snap off under such conditions. Also poor practice is a deeply cratered hole caused by careless drilling, since here again the anchor may be stressed rather than the surrounding rock (Fig-75). Where the rock is soft, like flowstone or sandstone for instance, the expansion cone may be driven into the base of a hole instead of the anchor and the sleeve not expand correctly. Also if the hole has been drilled sloppily or overlarge, the sleeve may not expand enough to grip the sides effectively. This type of anchor grips by stressing the surrounding rock (Fig-76), and will split it if located too close to cracks or edges or in thinly bedded rock.

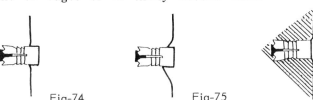

Fig-74   Fig-75   Fig-76

There is always the possibility of mechanical failure of the sleeve itself - such devices are after all only industrial fixings intended to support inanimate objects. Safety is only guaranteed by using multiple anchors - never trust your life to a single bolt.

MARKING ANCHORS

Existing anchors are inconspicuous and often difficult to locate, particularly in mid-pitch where the site of a rebelay or deviation may not be immediately obvious. Such anchors can be marked and made more noticeable. There are two methods, both carried out during installation as the anchor is being driven into its hole.

1/ A 5mm wide strip of any brightly coloured synthetic fabric has one end placed in the hole, trapped in position by the anchor (Fig-77).

2/ A suitable metal eyelet (such as those used in tackle sacks) is used to retain a coloured plastic disc or "washer". The eyelet/washer is placed in the hole and the Spit anchor driven through this to fix it in position (Fig-78).

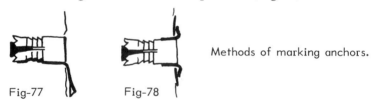

Methods of marking anchors.

Fig-77   Fig-78

MAINTENANCE

The useful life of a bolt anchor is indeterminate, dependent largely on location and frequency of use. The anchor permanently embedded in the cave wall is prone to corrosion if not maintained. The main enemies are water, mud, and neglect; the necessary maintenance minimal - simply greasing occasionally, although there are certain measures which can be taken during installation. Firstly - in a location which becomes wet from time to time, the anchor should be placed in slightly overhanging rock, or angled a little so as to be self-draining. Secondly - after driving the anchor into place, it is necessary to fill it with grease, so that as the first bolt is screwed in the grease is forced into the cracks and gaps at the rear of the anchor casing. These parts are damaged during insertion and need most protection from corrosion. Subsequently a light application of any waterproof grease every few trips is all that is needed. Some common sense is necessary - every group packing each anchor with grease on each trip is not harmful to the anchor, but soon becomes messy and ropes inevitably pick up surplus grease. Mud is particularly damaging to anchors, it aids corrosion and acts as an abradent, removing any plating from the threads as bolts are screwed in. It can be removed by a jet of water (squeezy bottle) followed by a blast of WD40 and a blob of grease. This is hardly too much trouble considering that a well placed (and maintained) anchor will continue to do its job for many years. With this in mind, it's best to carry bolt hangers in the tackle sack along with the rope, rather than dangling from the belt where they are inevitably ground along the walls, the threads getting damaged and covered in mud.

Anchors planted downwards into the rock are useless unless permanently fitted with a bolt and hanger (and packed with grease or epoxy resin) - left open they soon become clogged with silt or full of water and may be rendered unusable within weeks.

4.2 KNOTS

GENERAL POINTS

Since clearly it is always necessary to knot a rope to be able to use it, competence with the basic rigging knots and their application is a fundamental feature of caving technique. This simple, familiar act, so commonplace as to be almost taken for granted is in fact very important. The strongest rope and soundest anchors are of little practical value if attached by inadequate knots.

Obviously a caver should be certain of his ability - lives will depend on it. Knotting a couple of metres of old rope by the fireside is a pleasant way to spend long winter evenings and the practice will prove invaluable underground. Understanding the characteristics of a few simple knots will suffice for a lifetime of safe caving.

Every knot temporarily weakens the rope it is tied in; this is an inevitable consequence of distorting the rope over itself even though the effect varies according to the type of knot. In practice, it is as well to assume a 50% reduction in rope strength with the knots commonly used by cavers. Obviously this effect is not cumulative - a chain is always as strong as its weakest link.

TYPES - APPLICATIONS

Comparatively few knots are in fact necessary and these can be divided into two categories according to their common use; i.e. forming a loop for attachment, or for joining one rope to another.

68

LOOP KNOTS	JOINING KNOTS
1. Overhand Loop	9. Figure-8 Bend
2. Figure-8 Loop	10. Double Fisherman's
3. Figure-9 Loop	
4. Bowline	
5. Double Bowline	
6. Bowline on a Bight	
7. Butterfly Knot	
8. Capuchin Knot	

LOOP KNOTS

1. OVERHAND LOOP. The Overhand Knot is the most basic knot possible, simply a loop of rope with the end threaded through it. The Overhand Loop is exactly the same only tied in a doubled section of rope. Simple and foolproof, but comparatively weak and difficult to untie after being loaded (Fig-79).

Use: General purpose; Shock Absorption Knot.

Fig-79

2. FIGURE-8 LOOP. The traditional caver' knot, simple, strong and versatile, it lends itself to almost every purpose underground. Easier to untie after loading than the Overhand Loop (Fig-80).

Fig-80

FIGURE-8 LOOP (REVERSED). The same knot tied in a different fashion using the end of the rope (Fig-81) for attachment to a thread belay, or as a tie-in to a climber's harness.

Use: Multi-purpose; Rigging.

Fig-81

3. FIGURE-9 LOOP. Similar to the Figure-8 Loop but with an additional half-turn within the knot. Somewhat stronger, but bulkier and harder to untie after loading (Fig-82).

Use: Rigging, particularly lightweight (9mm dia.) rope where maximum strength retention is essential.

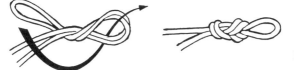

Fig-82

4. BOWLINE. A safe, simple knot used mainly for attaching the end of a rope to a thread belay. It has a tendency to work loose in very stiff or resilient ropes and should always be secured with a further knot, such as an Overhand Knot, tied on the same side as the rope end. The Bowline is a secure knot only if loaded along its major axis. Heavy sideways loading may distort it into a slip knot. However, it has two distinct advantages, the loop formed is easily adjusted and the knot is very easily untied even after heavy loading (Fig-83).

Use: Multi-purpose; General ropework; Traverse line attachment.

5. DOUBLE BOWLINE. The same knot tied in a double section of rope, generally for attachment mid-rope (Fig-84).

Use: Rigging; Thread belays in mid-rope.

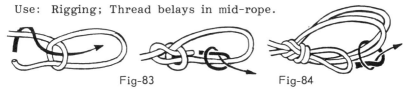

Fig-83   Fig-84

6. BOWLINE ON A BIGHT. A Bowline variation tied in a double rope (a bight) with the end loop passed over the partially completed knot. The result is a Bowline with two loops, each adjustable relative to the other (Fig-85).

Use: Rigging; Ring hanger attachment; Y-anchors; Shock Absorption Knot.

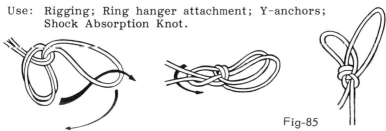

Fig-85

70

7. BUTTERFLY KNOT. A symetrical mid-rope loop knot, which may be loaded from the loop or along the standing rope in either direction. Easily adjusted and readily untied after use (Fig-86).

   Use: Rigging; Mid-rope traverse line attachment;
         Shock Absorption Knot.

Fig-86

8. CAPUCHIN KNOT. A comparatively little known knot, in effect half a Double Fisherman's tied in a doubled section of rope (Fig-87)

   Use: Stopper knot in the end of a rope; Blocking
         knot with the Cord Technique.

Fig-87

JOINING KNOTS

9. FIGURE-8 BEND. A different use of the (Reversed) Figure-8 Knot used to join the ends of two ropes of equal diameter very securely (Fig-88).

   Use: Joining ropes.

Fig-88

10. DOUBLE FISHERMAN'S BEND. Essentially two "stopper knots" tied in opposition to each other in the ends of separate ropes, designed to slide together forming the knot proper (Fig-89). This is a very secure knot often used for tying rope slings. It is prone to jamming under load and may have to be cut from the rope after particularly heavy loading. This tendency to jam, however, also has its positive side in that the knot will not work loose.

Use: Joining ropes; Rope slings.

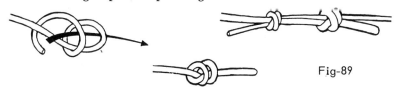

Fig-89

SAFETY LOOP

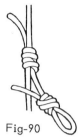

With SRT, whenever two ropes are joined in mid-pitch, a "safety loop" must be provided at the joining knot. This is for the caver to clip into for protection while making the manoeuvre to pass the knot (Fig-90). Here the tail of the rope above is left deliberately long and a loop knot tied in this to provide the necessary attachment.

Fig-90

BACK-UP KNOTS

All knots should be habitually checked and tightened before use (by everybody!). Any knot in the end of a rope should have a "tail" of at least 20cm sticking out of it and also be secured by an additional "back-up" knot such as an Overhand or half of a Double Fisherman's Bend - half-hitches are insufficient (see Fig-83). Whenever a knot is tied it is <u>always</u> worth the extra few seconds care it takes to tie a good one.

4.3 PACKING ROPES

SURFACE

Ropes are packed into the sack in the <u>reverse</u> order they will be required in the cave (i.e. last rope first) and the bags numbered in order of use.

The ropes can either be coiled and stuffed into the sacks, or packed loose in such a way that they can be drawn out without tangling; each method has certain advantages. The first is convenient for several short ropes of differing lengths which are more easily handled in separate coils. The second method is better for long ropes and for use on pitches where there may be loose rocks. In this case the sack is attached to the caver's belt, who feeds the rope out as he descends. Should he reach a ledge with loose rocks, he can simply kick them down the pitch without fear of damaging any gear below. Not having the weight of the rope dangling below also makes rigging easier. However, there are certain precautions to observe while packing the rope into the sack. It is <u>absolutely imperative</u> that a stopper knot is tied in the lower end; this is necessary to prevent inadvertent abseiling off the end should the rope prove too short. With the arrangement shown (Fig-91), the descender stops against the first knot and the second loop knot can be clipped into, or if necessary used to stand up in. Subsequently, a further length of rope can be added.

Fig-91

72

The rope is fed neatly into the sack avoiding making small coils which twist the rope and can cause it to tangle during the descent (Fig-92). This is easier if the sack is stiff enough to stand on its own, otherwise it can be hung from the caver's waistbelt.

Fig-92

UNDERGROUND

At the base of the pitch, any excess rope is either coiled and hung clear of the floor (Fig-93), or left in the sack which is suspended a short distance above the floor by its hauling loops (Fig-94). This precaution serves to keep the excess rope clean, avoids it being trodden on, and protects it from damage by falling rocks. Weighting the lower end of the rope also makes the initial few metres of climbing easier on the return.

Spare rope coiled at foot of pitch.

Fig-93

Excess rope packed in sack ready for hauling.

Fig-94

Hauling the rope up from the pitch head, it is less likely to snag with a streamlined tackle sack at its end than a coil of rope.

COILING ROPES

Ropes are generally only coiled for storage (see p. 52). Certain very stiff ropes which are not easily packed into sacks might be coiled for carrying around the shoulders and used on surface pitches. Here utmost care must be taken that the rope is not draped across a leaky miner's lamp battery. If the rope will not pack into a tackle sack, then don't take it underground.

4.4 RIGGING

Though often cloaked in mystique, rigging is simply the means of installing the equipment necessary to progress safely through the cave - for the most part involving no more than the common sense application of a few simple principles. However, it is a task to be approached responsibly and carried out conscientiously with some attention to detail. Here we cross the bounds of fun and expediency - lives are at stake.

Given suitable equipment, it is the style of rigging which largely determines:

- The safety of the caving team.

- The speed and ease of climbing.

- Wear and tear on the equipment.

Pitch rigging is hardly an exact science, each pitch presents a particular set of technical problems which can be resolved in a number of different ways, according to individual needs and conditions at the time. However, for those who appreciate clear guidelines, there are three basic rules which should be strictly adhered to:-

- Two anchors at the top of each pitch.

- Eliminate abrasion.

- Minimise any shock load.

The basic ways and means of achieving these objectives are explained in the following pages. Understand however that an important aspect of pitch rigging, and one easily lost amongst these dry, technical considerations, is that safety is ultimately a function of character and plain common sense. From the outset it is vital to learn not to compromise safety for the sake of expediency, whatever its guise. Although having once accepted this constraint, there are no technical problems met underground which cannot be overcome by suitable rigging.

GENERAL CONSIDERATIONS

As a starting point, consider the rope rigged in the pitch as a succession of linked elements, starting with the rock, then the anchor, bolt, hanger, and the rope itself. Each of these elements having particular characteristics, different strengths and weaknesses depending on how it is used. Obviously, the whole system is only as strong as the weakest of these elements. Therefore as each individual pitch presents a different set of considerations, it is necessary not only to use safe equipment but

74

to have some understanding of its capabilities in order to be able
to use it appropriately. In fact, the whole basis of rope rigging is
simply ensuring that you stay within the very specific limits
imposed by the equipment; stray outside these limits and you are
in mortal danger.

In arranging an anchor for the rope, there are four main
requirements:

1. The rig must be strong and secure enough to withstand the
    forces involved in the worst shock-load (that is as strong as
    the knotted rope itself).

2. Provide a free hang to eliminate abrasion.

3. As far as possible, avoid objective hazards such as water or
    stone fall.

4. Facilitate easy access at the pitch head.

Rarely will a single anchor of any type fulfill all of these
requirements. Consequently, the first rule of rigging is:-

TWO SEPARATE ANCHORS AT THE TOP OF EACH PITCH.

Fig-95 - Back-up, traverse and main belays.

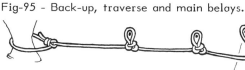

TRAVERSE LINE

Wherever reaching the hang point for the main rope
involves climbing out over the pitch, a traverse line
should be installed for safety. This is rigged at about
head height (in order to minimise the effect of a slip),
linking a safe back-up belay to the main belay
(Fig 95). The traverse line provides both a back-up to
the main belay and a safeguard for getting on and off
the rope. In such cases, protection is necessary for the
caver rigging the rope and the technique used to
arrange this is very simple.

Once attached to the back-up belay the rope is
used by the rigger to protect himself while installing
the main belay. He can do this with an auto-lock
descender, an ordinary descender by tying a knot in
the rope beneath it, or a safety-cord clipped into a
loop tied in the rope. Should he then fall (and he must
take whatever precautions are necessary to ensure that
he does not!), the force on the belay is not very great
because of the pendulum nature of the fall, although
the caver might get bashed about a bit on the way.

TYPES

There are two distinct types of traverse line, one where the rope is used for protection in an exposed situation (Fig-96), and a second case where the rope is used for aid - to hang from while crossing a blank wall for example (Fig-97). This distinction is important: Where the rope is used solely for protection the distance between belay points is rather less critical, generally they can be further apart. Also, as the rope is not loaded and so unlikely to be abraded, it is acceptable if it rounds a bend and/or rests lightly against the rock.

Fig-96
Traverse line
for protection.

Fig-97
Traverse line
for direct aid.

The traverse line used for aid is a different matter, here the caver hangs from the rope supported by his safety-cords, so the distance between belays and the degree of tension in the rope are crucial. Because the rope is loaded, it must not be allowed to touch the rock or it will abrade. Rigging such a line, the caver hangs from the belay loop by his long safety-cord, and braced out at an angle to the wall fixes the rope to the next belay with as little slack as possible (Fig-98). He then attaches his short safety-cord to this section, transfers the long safety-cord to the next belay loop and repeats the process. Those following progress by using both safety-cords on the rope, leaving the longer one clipped to a section as the shorter one is transferred to the next.

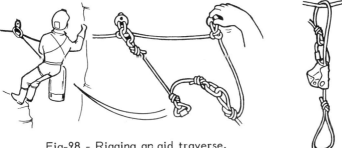

Fig-98 - Rigging an aid traverse.

Fig-99

The footloop jammer passed over the traverse line and clipped into its cord upside down (Fig-99) provides an adjustable stirrup, useful for passing intermediate anchors on a blank wall.

WARNING

It is vitally important for the caver never to climb up above a traverse line. Falling from this position the fall-factor is always high (even if only the length of a safety-cord) and by loading a horizontally tensioned rope in this manner the forces created are amplified and very likely to break it.

MAIN ANCHOR

The purpose of the main anchor is to locate the pitch rope in the optimum position to avoid loose rocks or falling water, and provide a free hang for as far as possible without the rope touching the rock - in other words, out over the pitch.

Obviously the back-up belay must be strong enough to support the rope should the main belay fail, which is not to say that the main belay is any less important. The "main" belay is just that, and as such must be designed to minimise the possibility of serious failure. Here unless a really sound anchor can be found, two separate anchors are used and the chance of both of these failing simultaneously is very low. It is foolhardy ever to trust your life to a single bolt.

DOUBLE ANCHORS

A common rather outdated arrangement is to place two anchors one above the other, with the connecting rope tied with minimal slack (Fig-100). The upper anchor will take a shock load should the lower tail, but this will be insignificant. There is, however, little point in having two anchors and loading only one. Often a better arrangement is to load both anchors so that each takes less than the full load. Together they are less likely to fail and will not produce a shock-load in any case (Fig-101).

Fig-100 - Superimposed double anchor.

Fig-101 - Shared double anchor.

The best arrangement of all is a Y-anchor, where both anchors are loaded about equally, generally on opposing walls with the actual hang point being somewhere in between (Fig-102). This technique is particularly useful in caves with narrow, twisting stream canyons cutting down into the pitch, where it may be impossible to obtain a free hang from either wall. So that each arm of the belay is under no more strain than the main rope, the angle between the two must never exceed 120°. Also, since generally bolt hangers are not designed to work at more than 45° to the rock, an angle of 90° between the two is the working rule (Fig-103). In practice, this is easy to recognise and in this case each arm of the belay is subject to about 70% of the load on the main rope.

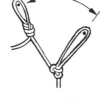

Fig-102 - Y-anchor.　　　　　Fig-103 - Safe loading angle.

BOLT HANGERS

As a general rule, the choice of which type of bolt hanger to use is largely determined by the location of the anchor and configuration of the belay (see Fig-69). At Lizard, we use two types: Ring and Bollard style hangers, fixed almost exclusively with Bowline on a Bight and Butterfly knots.

The normal method is to thread sufficient Ring hangers for the pitch onto the rope before it is tied to the initial belay, so that they slide freely along the rope as it is pulled from the sack. Bollard hangers are carried on a large karabiner clipped to the harness. Subsequently the caver chooses the appropriate hanger at each belay point - Bollards for back-up, traverses, and certain offset Y-anchors, Rings for Y-anchors, roof bolts and rebelays. The Ring hangers are utilised as needed simply by tying them directly into the knots (Fig-104). Any spare rings are removed at the foot of the pitch and threaded onto the next rope.

Two methods
of tying on
Ring hangers.

Fig-104

INTERMEDIATE ANCHORS

Having constructed the main belay, the caver descends and at
each point where the rope touches the rock, he installs an
intermediate anchor (rebelay) at or immediately beneath the rub
point so that the rope again hangs free below it (Fig-105). This is
necessary in order to avoid the otherwise inevitable damage to the
rope arising from contact with the rock while loaded, doubtless the
most serious single hazard of rope rigging. Thus the second rule:-

ELIMINATE ABRASION.

No amount of abrasion, however slight, is acceptable.

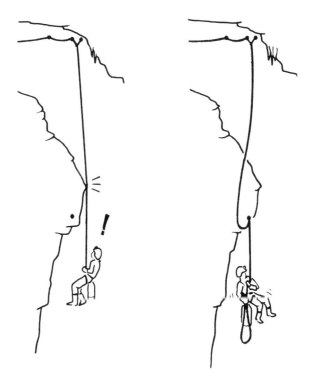

Fig-105 - Intermediate anchor.

Due to the receding perspective in a pitch it is often difficult
to decide exactly where the rope will hang below. Pull some rope
from the sack, hold it against the proposed anchor point and see
if it touches further down. Alternatively, drop a stone from this
point and watch (and listen) if it hits the wall.

At intermediate anchors, a single bolt is usually sufficient, as the rebelay is effectively backed-up by the main belay. It is necessary to leave a loop of slack rope at this point so that those following can install their descenders. The length of this loop is important and is best kept to a minimum, particularly close to the pitch head, for should the intermediate anchor fail, a shock-load will be transmitted to the belay above. About 1m is sufficient, but the elasticity of the rope must be taken into account when determining this amount or the loop may disappear when unloaded. With some experience it is possible to estimate the amount of slack quite accurately on short pitches. On a long pitch it is better to unload the rope as follows:

- Fix a Ring hanger to the anchor and attach a karabiner or 7mm M/R, or use a plate hanger with a large attachment hole or one equipped with two karabiners or M/Rs.

- Clip into the hanger or upper M/R with the short safety-cord and then feed rope through the descender until entirely supported by the safety-cord – do not remove the descender at this stage but lock it off instead (Fig-106).

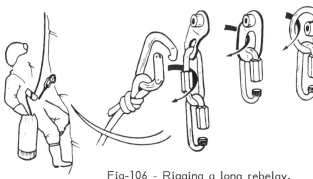
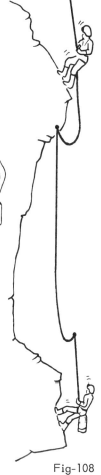

Fig-106 - Rigging a long rebelay.

- Tie a knot about 50cm below the descender and clip this to the remaining karabiner leaving exactly the right amount of slack. Transfer the descender in the normal way and continue down.

The technique of rebelaying is continued to the foot of the pitch, whether the rope is simply touching the rock or there are a series of separate drops close together.

Fig-108

80

JOINING ROPES

Normally each pitch is rigged with a single length of rope. Where this is not the case, the separate ropes are, wherever possible, joined at intermediate anchor points to avoid passing knots unnecessarily. The second rope is tied through a loop formed in the upper rope so that should the attachment karabiner or M/R fail, the ropes remain joined together. Any spare rope is coiled and hung close to the anchor to avoid abseiling down the wrong rope (Fig-107). This should be done without untying the end knot.

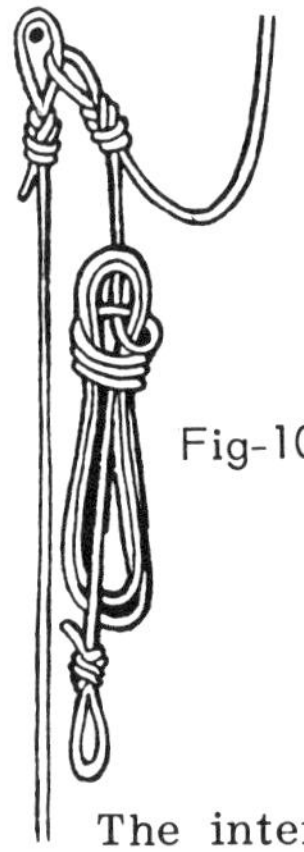

Fig-107

Where a substantial ledge or a traverse requires more than a small amount of slack to be left in the rope, the continuing pitch must be rigged with a double belay to avoid the fall and/or abrasion point which would result from the failure of a single anchor.

The intermediate anchor technique has other advantages apart from avoiding abrasion and/or water. Splitting the pitch into sections reduces bounce in the rope and because the rope is attached to several anchors overall safety is enhanced. Speed is substantially increased because now several of the team can descend or climb simultaneously, provided each is hanging from a separate anchor (Fig-108 p.79).

4.5 SUPPLEMENTARY TECHNIQUES

CABLE TETHERS

Tethers are short lengths (between 0.5 and 2m) of stainless or galvanised steel cable (breaking load 750-1000kg) with a swaged loop at each end. They are used for rebelaying the rope in the isolated circumstances where the nature of the rock (thinly bedded, shaley) precludes placing an anchor at the correct location (i.e. at or just beneath the potential abrasion point). The tether is attached to an anchor above the rebelay point and used to extend the fixing to a position where the rope will hang clear of the rock (Fig-109). Tethers remain largely unaffected by friction against rock, it is the rock which suffers in this case. However, because of its extremely low stretch, steel cable has no capacity to absorb a shock-load, consequently it is important to ensure that in passing the rebelay the lower end of the tether is not raised above its normal position. Once favoured for rigging ladders, tethers are rarely carried and this technique seldom used.

Fig-109

Cable tether.

ROPE PROTECTORS

In certain circumstances the rope can be protected from abrasion against the rock by a rope protector - a sheath of tough, abrasion resistant fabric fastened around the rope with a strip of "Velcro" and fixed in place with a piece of string (Fig-110). Each caver must remove the sheath to pass and replace it in exactly the right position. Protecting the rope in this fashion is only likely to prove acceptable close to the anchor at the top of a pitch, there an empty tackle sack will often do the job, although care must be taken to ensure that the rope cannot move sideways onto the rock. The rope should follow as gentle a curve as possible and not be led over a sharp edge. Nowadays this rather outdated "padding" technique is most often used during initial prospection, when one caver descends to check if the shaft is blocked at the bottom and not worth bolting properly. Used on a normal trip, particularly in mid-pitch, it's a crude technique which usually turns out to be more trouble than it's worth.

Fig-110

DEVIATION

A useful alternative method of redirecting the rope on a pitch so as to avoid an abrasion hazard, waterfall, or a particularly narrow section, is the technique of deviation.

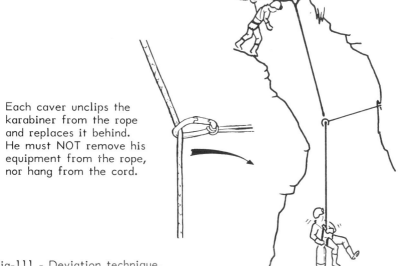

Each caver unclips the karabiner from the rope and replaces it behind. He must NOT remove his equipment from the rope, nor hang from the cord.

Fig-111 - Deviation technique.

Here an anchor, perhaps on the opposite wall, is used to deflect the rope away from its normal vertical hang by means of a length of cord and a karabiner clipped around the rope (Fig-111). Each caver unclips this in order to pass and replaces it behind him. The caver's equipment (descender, jammers) is not taken off the rope, as a result the manoeuvre is quick and easy, and uses less rope than a rebelay. The force transferred to such a belay is not very great as the rope is not directly fixed into it and a shock-load would not result should it fail. Thus many belays are suitable for deviations which would be extremely dangerous if used for rebelays - for instance, a smallish stalagmite, a knot jammed in a crack, or a piton. However, some discretion is needed. Always bear in mind that rigging a deviation to an insecure flake, for example, could cause it to become detached and injure those below. Furthermore, where failure of a deviation could cause the rope to take up a dangerous line, be abraded as a result of the ensuing pendulum, or leave the climber beneath a heavy waterfall, the deviation belay should be a bolt or a sound natural anchor and a substantial cord used.

Note that the more a rope is diverted from the vertical, the more strain is applied to the deviation and the more difficult it is to pass.

The illustration (Fig-112) shows a deviation cord fitted with a special lightweight bolt hanger. The cords are 1m circumference loops of 5mm dia. low-stretch cord, tied with a Double Fisherman's knot and equipped with an alloy snaplink. They can be shortened by tying an Overhand knot and lengthened by "larks-footing" two or more together.

Fig-112 - Deviation hanger.

PENDULUMS

It is not always necessary to descend a pitch directly beneath the main belay. The technique of rebelay and deviation can be used to arrange an oblique line of descent in order to reach a particular objective (a high level passage in the shaft), or to avoid a hazard (e.g. an area of loose rock or a waterfall).

Often it is possible to make a so-called "tension traverse" to reach the necessary anchor points simply by using holds on the wall to pull across sideways while suspended from above. The alternative is penduluming, swinging to and fro on the rope until sufficient amplitude is gained to reach the objective (Fig-113). To succeed, this technique depends on the ratio of distance down the pitch to sideways deflection not being excessive. Experience shows the practical limit to be about 5-1, which means that to easily reach an objective 4 metres away, there must be about 20m of rope above. There are two particular dangers: smashing into the wall, and much worse the risk of the loaded rope above being cut by sharp rock while swinging. It is absolutely essential to check that the rope hangs completely clear of the rock, and throughout the manoeuvre another caver should also be in a position to verify this from above.

A stopper knot tied in the rope at the correct level makes the manoeuvre easier to repeat for those following. From this position it is a simple matter to pull across using the fixed rope.

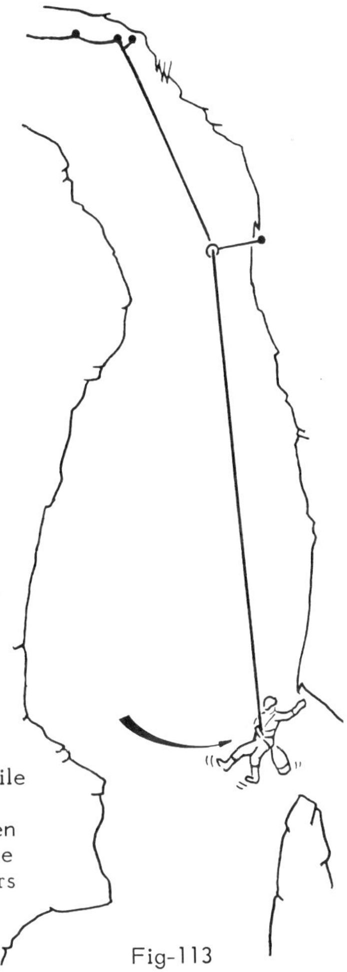

It is very difficult to initiate a swing while hanging in mid-air. A makeshift grapnel (hammer tied on a length of cord) is often useful in these circumstances. This can be thrown to lodge behind a flake or boulders on a ledge and used to reach a wall.

Fig-113

AVOIDING SHOCK-LOADS

The basic techniques outlined above will serve for most caves, but there are situations where ingenuity is called for and there is generally plenty of scope for this, provided that one simple guideline is strictly adhered to: Because the rope used for SRT is of low-stretch construction it has only a limited capacity to absorb energy, it must therefore never be subject to the shock-load arising from a fall-factor of any significance. There is a danger here of becoming lost in conjecture; nevertheless, a degree of understanding of these dry, theoretical ideas is important if the rope is to be rigged safely and at the risk of repetition:-

The fall-factor is a simple concept used to describe the relationship between the length of a fall and the amount of rope available to intercept it. Briefly, the energy of a falling body is proportional to the distance fallen, while the rope's capacity to absorb this energy is proportional to its length. By dividing the one by the other, we arrive at a fall-factor which, for our purposes, can be said to vary between 0 and 2. Note that it is the relationship between these two factors which is most important, not their value. Take the case of a fall-factor 1 fall (Fig-51, p. 47), that is where the distance fallen and the length of rope are equal, say someone falling from the head of a pitch onto a slack rope. The shock would be substantial, but a 2m fall onto 2m of rope produces more or less the same shock-load in the rope as a 10m fall onto 10m of rope, the fall-factor being identical in both cases. With many SRT ropes, this "peak impact load" is likely to be in the region of 700/800kg, which is coming uncomfortably close to the limitations of both the equipment and the force a caver might withstand without catastrophic damage. Now envisage the same situation but in this instance the caver has climbed the length of the slack rope up above the pitch and then fallen. He will of course fall twice the distance but with only the same amount of rope to absorb the much greater forces produced. This equates to about a fall-factor 2 - a very high factor which would almost certainly break the rope, or the belay, and definitely break the caver!

Third rule: <u>MINIMISE ANY POSSIBLE SHOCK-LOADS.</u>

However, once aware of this absolute limitation of a low-stretch rope, there is some scope for improvisation. It is usually possible to avoid dangerous situations arising by simply ensuring that the main belay is always positioned at a level below the back-up belay. This being so, even a fall-factor 1 becomes impossible and in most cases no more than a violent swing will result. <u>Do not forget</u>, however, that as a result of this swing the rope could be cut against a sharp edge or the caver smashed against the wall!

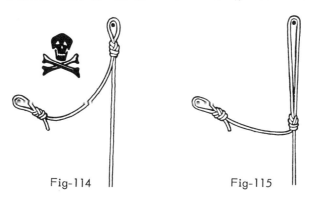

Fig-114   Fig-115

This procedure (main–belay below back-up) is not inviolate, take the situation in Fig-114 where in order to ensure a free hang the main anchor is placed well above the previous one. This is potentially a very dangerous configuration - should the upper anchor fail with the caver close to it, a fall-factor of around 2 would result. Even here we can make things safe by tying a loop knot at a point below the level of the previous anchor (Fig-115). This ensures that the descender/jammers are installed at a low enough level and reduces the fall-factor to almost nothing.

SHOCK ABSORPTION KNOTS

There are still certain rare situations where in spite of all that can be done to reduce the fall-factor, a considerable shock-load will still be placed on the rope should the main belay fail. Nevertheless, all is not lost. We can take steps to mitigate the resulting shock-load by the judicious use of "shock-absorbing" knots (Fig-116).

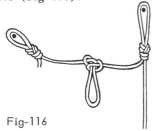

Fig-116

The principle at work here is simple, certain loop knots (notably the Overhand, Butterfly and Bowline on a Bight) tied in the unloaded section of rope (traverse line) will, if loaded, slip a little and in doing so both absorb a certain amount of energy and also release additional rope to help minimise the shock (Fig-117). This is a sensible precaution to take with thin (9mm dia.) ropes.

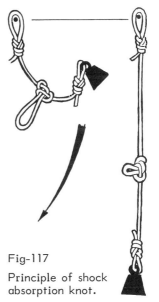

Fig-117

Principle of shock absorption knot.

4.6 WET PITCHES

Most of the caves in Britain are active, the climate wet, and consequently many pitches contain waterfalls of varying volume, anything from a refreshing spray to a thundering torrent.

Contrary to a tradition of caving in rubber diving suits, with guidebook descriptions of "classic sporting descents" made directly in the path of the falling water, make no mistake that <u>wet pitches constitute the most difficult and dangerous obstacles normally met underground</u>. They should be approached warily, and as a general rule with the rope rigged as far away from the water as possible.

HAZARDS

Apart from hazards arising from flooding and wear and tear on equipment caused directly by the water (reciprocation of rope against sharp rock), climbing a very wet pitch is dangerous in itself. It is strenuous and uncomfortable climbing up against the weight of falling water (the effect is much more evident while climbing than descending). Even routine rope manoeuvres are difficult while blinded, half-drowned and numbed by cold. Anyone stuck in mid-rope is soon prey to hypothermia, the rate of heat loss due to the wind chill effect is tremendous, and rescue may prove impractical. Common sense should be enough to realise that the worst place to descend a wet pitch is that already occupied by the waterfall. Every effort should be made to rig the rope clear of the path taken by the water, even under flood conditions when it spurts further out into the shaft.

SPECIAL TECHNIQUES

There are a number of steps that can be taken to avoid waterfalls; the simplest is traversing out at the pitch head.

- Due to the natural tendency of a stream to cut a canyon down into the pitch, there are often remnant high-level fossil routes (or at least ledges) leading out over the pitch to a point where the rope can be hung completely clear of the water. Failing this, it should be possible to climb (using artificial techniques if the walls are blank) out to a suitable point. A traverse line is fixed for those following and generally this method, supplemented as necessary by the next two, turns out to be the best solution.

- Further down a pitch it may be possible to pendulum out across the wall and install one or more rebelays or deviations clear of the waterfall. In the case of deviations, the rope should be fixed at the foot of the pitch so that those following can pull across to the deviation without having to repeat the pendulum.

- In certain pitches, once a caver has descended, he can anchor the rope at the bottom so that it is pulled diagonally away from the water. It's rather difficult to abseil on a rope rigged this way, but climbing is less of a problem, particularly if one leg is hooked over the rope (Fig-118). This technique can be much improved if a second rope is available to rig a taut, sloping guide-line alongside the main rope. It's then just a matter of descending and climbing the main rope as normal but with a safety-cord (and pulley?) clipped to the guide-line (Fig-119). With both these techniques (unless the guide-line is left in position), the first caver down and last one up usually get a soaking!

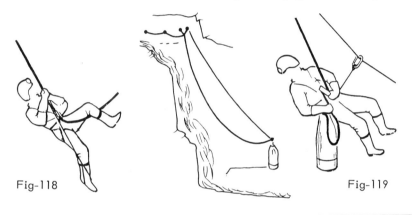

Fig-118   Fig-119

4.7 DE-RIGGING

Obviously the pitch is detackled by the last man to ascend, but as soon as his tackle sack is full, he either passes this equipment on, or leap-frogs the rest of the team and heads out of the cave, leaving the tackle on subsequent pitches to someone else.

During de-rigging, all knots, hangers, etc. are left in place on the rope which is simply stuffed into the sack and sorted out later when the rope is washed and returned to the store. There is nothing to be gained by messing about with this sort of job underground, and it slows the task of de-rigging.

At each stage of the ascent, excess rope is pulled up and packed into the sack which is then secured to the rope. This serves to protect the rope from any possible damage by falling rocks, and also minimises the likelihood of it snagging while being hauled up the pitch. If a distinctive knot is made in the rope at the foot of each pitch, the individual pitch lengths can be measured and rope and rigging requirements recorded for future trips (see App 1).

HAULING

As a general rule it is far more efficient to carry gear up pitches than involve another operation hauling it up from the top. Light sacks are carried clipped to the side of the harness/belt, heavier ones are best dangled beneath the Delta M/R on a cord. Hauling is only necessary in a very deep cave where there are too many sacks and the individual loads too heavy to climb with. Where hauling is unavoidable, a second rope is used, and a separate lighter line might be considered for this purpose (8mm dia. polypropylene), which saves wear and tear on SRT rope. A simple pulley/jammer arrangement makes hauling much less strenuous (Fig-120) and a handled jammer is more comfortable while pulling on the rope.

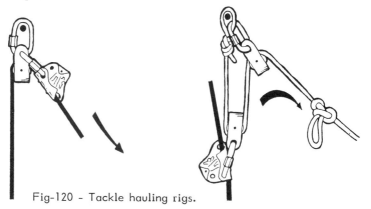

Fig-120 - Tackle hauling rigs.

If it is sufficiently long, the sacks are best attached to the centre of the rope, and the lower section used as a guide-line to help free any snags and to pull the rope back down the pitch. In a restricted pitch, the sacks should be spaced at intervals along a section of rope. There is considerable danger to those below from falling rocks dislodged by the tackle sacks, and an alternative technique is for the last caver to climb alongside the sacks and deal with any problems as he de-rigs the main rope. However, in order to be safe from falling rock, he must always remain above the sacks, clip a safety-cord around the haul line to prevent the sacks swinging away and jamming where he cannot reach them, and the hauling team must follow his directions.

Tackle transport is essentially a rather loose discipline with as many variations as there are caves and trips into them, but it is important to ensure that each caver carries his share and huge amounts of equipment are not left to those at the rear.

APPENDIX — 1

ADDRESS LIST

BRITISH CAVE RESEARCH ASSOCIATION
Secretary - R.G. Willis
BCM
British Cave Research Assn.
LONDON   WC1N 3XX

NATIONAL CAVING ASSOCIATION
3 Valletort Road
Stoke
PLYMOUTH   PL1 5PH

Initial contact address for regional bodies, i.e.,

Council of Northern Caving Clubs   Derbyshire Caving Association
Council of Southern Caving Clubs   Cambrian Caving Council

NCA administers a number of committees, including an Equipment Committee dealing with any equipment related problems, and a Training Committee which runs an instructor certification scheme.

The Cave Instructor Certificate Scheme

The C.I.C. is an award designed for those such as outdoor centre instructors who regularly take parties into a variety of caves. It requires a wide and varied caving background and is not designed for non-specialists who should turn their attention to the more limited scope of the Local Cave Leader Assessment Scheme.

The scheme is likely to appeal to two different groups:-

(1) Cavers or Club Leaders who are interested in passing their skills on to others. For many, training is an end in itself, there is no obligation or requirement to progress to an assessment course.

(2) Those working towards the Cave Instructor Certificate, to satisfy Local Authorities/employers, etc., that they have undergone training and have been independently assessed as being suitably competent, before taking responsibility for the lives of others.

A significant part of the C.I.C. scheme involves the establishment of high standards in the practice and teaching of modern vertical caving techniques. Cavers attending C.I.C. Training Courses need to be already proficient in the use of SRT.

APPENDIX — 2

RIGGING TOPOS

Single Rope Techniques indicate the need for a different approach to planning tackle requirements. Much of the information contained in existing British guidebooks refers to outmoded techniques and is virtually useless in this respect. The two examples provided serve both to show how these caves might be rigged using SRT, and a simple graphic means of recording the information.

The necessary details are readily gained – during derigging all knots are left in the ropes and a distinctive knot tied at the foot of each pitch. Subsequently traverse line and individual pitch lengths are measured against two pegs set 10 metres apart with the distance between marked in metres. All knots are then untied and the total length of rope for each section measured. Later the rigging is drawn up according to a suitable scale and sufficient detail of the cave sketched around it to identify its positioning.

Rather lengthy written descriptions are also provided here, but in practice these should prove unnecessary for most caves.

TOPO SYMBOLS

● Bolt Anchor   ▲ Spike or Flake

O Natural Anchor   s O Natural Anchor & Sling

 Deviation |24 Pitch Length

40 Total Rope Length   **35** Rope Length to this Point

Rowten Pot (-105m) SD 098 780. Alt. 360m.

Although a large surface feature, most of the entrance hole is floored by huge blocks a few metres down, where a sizeable stream enters from Rowten Caves, cascading down a green and slippery gully before entering the main shaft. Predictably, following the watercourse has little to commend it, particularly as the main shaft can be reached directly from an adjacent "eyehole" entrance. This is a smaller opening immediately to the south, separated from the larger surface hole by a rock bridge.

SURFACE PITCH
Two permanent rawlbolts set into bedrock provide an initial belay, dropping over the lip to a rebelay some 3 metres down, clearing a pitch of 17m which lands on a large platform overlooking the main shaft (50m). This point can also be reached from the floor of the larger surface hole by a short pitch (5m) and crawling along an exposed ledge above the stream gully.

MAINSHAFT ROUTES
Various routes descend the main shaft – each reflecting a different stage in the development of vertical techniques as applied to this particular cave.

- Behind boulders to the right of the shaft, a steep gully drops to an old rawlbolt anchor above a pitch of 30 metres, a traditional ladder route descending against the wall to meet the stream on a wet and windy ledge 15 metres from the bottom of the shaft.

- An early SRT route leading over the nearside edge of the main shaft, follows two short pitches out to a prominent nose of rock, providing a free hanging pitch again of about 30 metres. This pitch is wet towards the bottom and lands on the same draughty ledge, from where a common pitch of 15 metres descends more or less alongside the waterfall to the shaft floor.

- RIFT ROUTE. To the left, a traverse crosses an exposed rock bridge spanning the stream gully where it enters the main shaft, onto a comfortable if muddy ledge. This point can be reached directly using deviations to redirect the rope on the surface pitch. The traverse line is continued to the far end of the ledge, where a high Y-anchor provides a short initial descent to a rebelay about 3 metres down, immediately above a widening rift heading back beneath the ledge. It is necessary to swing into this rift at a point some 4 metres below the rebelay. There are small footholds here which offer a stance of sorts as the rope is anchored a short way into the rift. Rigging between both walls from here provides a spectacular, airy pitch of 40 metres to the foot of the shaft. Continuing diagonally downwards into the rift for a few metres reaches an alternative hang above a pitch of 38 metres, farther away from the waterfall and closer to the subsequent pitches; either way it's an impressive descent.

ROWTEN POT

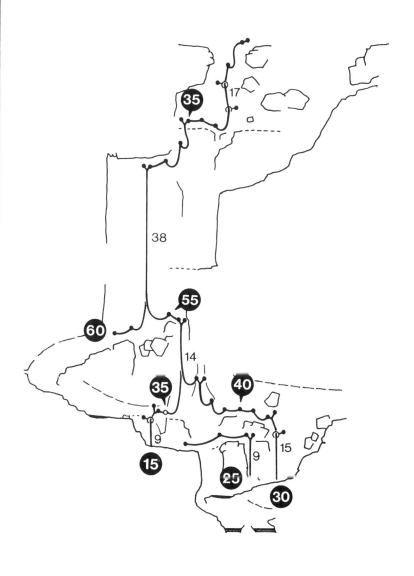

LOWER PITCHES

Below the main shaft the stream spills over a waterfall beneath huge poised blocks with alternative Third pitches to both right and left. To the right, stepping across a deep hole between boulders (traverse line) leads into a fossil by-pass with two short, arguably (though awkward) free-climbable pitches, doubling back beneath to regain the stream at the Fourth pitch (9m). The left alternative is more direct, rigged from an alcove with a false floor of jammed boulders in a free-hanging pitch of about 20 metres. The landing is on a ledge above a cascade with the head of the Fourth pitch (9m) a few metres upstream. Here the rope is anchored high from the only rock available and uses a deviation rigged from the opposite wall. The pitch lands in a pool and shortly beyond the stream disappears into a waterfall pitch, by-passed on the left by a traverse up onto fallen blocks followed by an alternative dry pitch of about 9 metres into the final chamber. Below, the passage loops around to meet the stream at a deep pool beneath the waterfall and continues beyond to a sump. There are in fact two sump pools divided by a ridge of rock. The smaller "upstream" sump eventually enters "Frakes Series" while the larger pool of the "downstream" sump emerges in Kingsdale Master Cave.

FLYOVER ROUTE

From a point 12 metres down the (left-hand) Third pitch, swinging across the shaft reaches a cross rift overlooking the streamway below the Fourth pitch. Rigging between the walls, succeeded by a rebelay further into the rift, gains a comfortable ledge and a high level by-pass to the lower active pitches. The by-pass requires a traverse line and continues over boulders and holes in the floor to a 15m pitch dropping into the Final chamber.

Descending the main shaft by the Rift Route and following the Flyover by-pass in the lower section of the cave, it is possible to rig safely down to the Final chamber in very wet conditions.

Diccan Pot (-105m) SD 775 757. Alt. 350m.

One of the traditional "sporting" descents and consequently the scene of many a sorry ordeal. Though short, this cave is very active, it is entirely unsuitable for the technically semi-skilled and extremely dangerous in high water conditions.

FIRST PITCH

The wide, low streamway gains height at a chute into a pool, succeeded by a stretch of stooping passage and a second deeper pool close to the First Pitch (35m). The pitch is rigged from a substantial thread well back from the lip and to spits at roof level. Here the stream spills into the shaft and cascades over a ledge 5m down, but with a dry section in the corner of the shaft where the rope can be rigged clear of the water. A fixed guideline is useful in wet conditions, the waterfall avoided simply by clipping a short safety-cord to the line while descending to the ledge. Here the rope is hung from a flake of rock, with a deviation about halfway down, to direct the rope away from the water when necessary.

SECOND AND THIRD PITCHES

The landing is on a large, spray-lashed platform with a deep pool in the middle and the Second Pitch (8m) following immediately, rigged from a massive thread where the shaft wall is undercut. A boulder-floored rift continues to two short consecutive pitches (counted together as the Third Pitch), rigged clear of the water by bridging out at a higher level, landing close to the Fourth and final pitch (35m).

FOURTH PITCH

This pitch is heavily watered, steep rather than vertical and broken by ledges into a series of cascades, or raging torrents depending on water levels. There is grave danger lurking here from hidden snags, sharp flakes beneath the water, cold, lack of communication, even drowning. The only safe solution in such places is to take a line of descent completely clear of the water at the farther side of the shaft. From here the surroundings are spectacular and the objective dangers largely removed.

Initially a traverse, rigged along the left wall, leads out over the stream gully to where the ledges peter out and make it necessary to crouch and rig a low anchor for the first part of the descent. About 10m down a rather steep pendulum is required to reach the far side of the shaft and establish a clear hang for the next section. A fixed line bolted across the shaft wall at this point aids this manoeuvre and avoids swinging back beneath the waterfall. The route then descends obliquely via two rebelays some 5 metres apart and on opposite walls of the shaft. A little further down a deviation directs the rope onto a ledge some 12 metres below, with a further rebelay for the remaining section of 8m to the foot of the shaft. The landing is in the final passageway of Alum Pot close to the terminal sump.

DICCAN POT

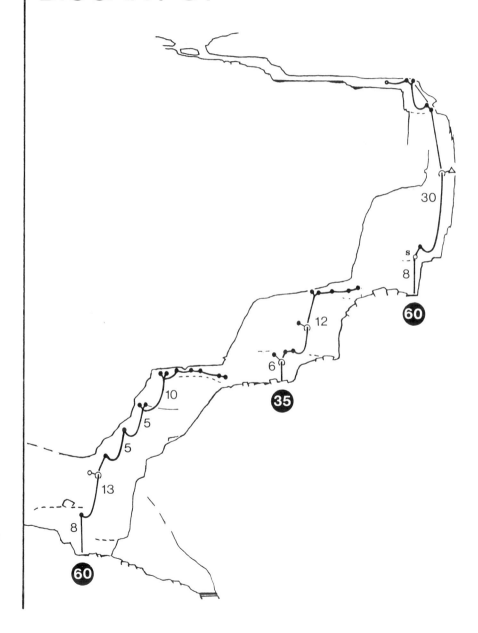

Lizard
Speleo-Systems

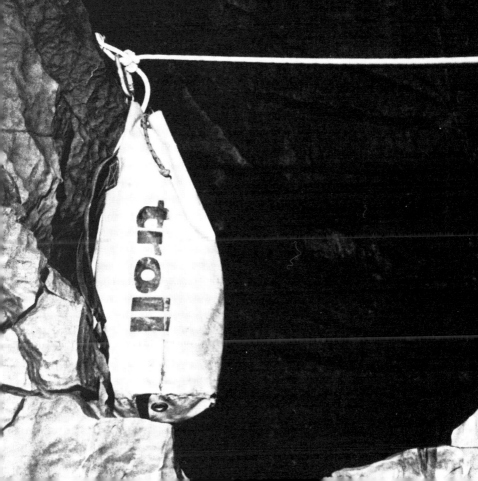